INSIGHT *Pocket* GUIDES

PARIS

PARIS

FRANCE

50p

D0452826

APA PUBLICATIONS

Dear Visitor!

Besides being perhaps the best preserved and grandest city in the world, Paris is a major hub of intellectual, cultural and artistic pursuits. It is loved universally for its cuisine, wine, fashion, painting, theatre and museums. 'If a man fell out of the moon into the town of Paris,' said G. K. Chesterton in 1908, 'he would know that it was the capital of a great nation.'

 Grace Coston, our correspondent in the city, is not from the moon but from America. 'Even after 10 years here I am still discovering more about Paris every day,' she says. Grace has worked here as a writer, translator, teacher, and now mother to bilingual children. 'I can firmly say that I wouldn't live anywhere else, and my enthusiasm for the city is even greater than it was when I first arrived.'

Grace's enthusiasm for Paris, combined with her writer's instincts and outsider's eye, makes her an ideal correspondent for Insight Guides. Her enthusiasm illuminates her carefully-devised itineraries that fill the main part of this book. These routes include all the essential sights, as well as Grace's own favourite corners of what is a fairly compact city. Each has Grace's own personal selection of cafés and restaurants.

In addition, she has created four day-trips to well-known destinations such as Versailles and Euro Disney, and to less visited ones such as Monet's house and garden in Normandy. 'This book is a way of showing off my home town,' says Grace. 'And any friend of Paris is a friend of mine.'

So welcome to Paris – and let Grace show you the best of the city.

Hans Höfer
Publisher, Insight Guides

C O N T E N T S

Pages 2/3:
Eiffel Tower
from
Trocadéro

*Pages 10/11:
Looking down on
the Seine*

Paris

0,5 miles / 800 m

Porte de Champerret
P.TE DE CHAMP
Boul. Berthier
Boul. Péreire
Rue Jouffroy
Boul.
Rue de Rome

Place du mal Juin
PÉREIRE
Av.
St. Francois de Sales
de

St Pierre
Av. des Ternes
WAGRAM

Boul. Victor Hugo
Boul. Couvion
Péreire
Av. Niel
Av. de Wagram
Rue de
COURCELLES
Boul. de Courcelles

Villiers
Boul. des
VILLIERS
Rue d
Malesherbes
Constantin

Pte Maillot
Palais des Congrès
Av. des Ternes
MONCEAU
Musée Nissim de Camondo
EUR

Avenue Charles de Gaulle
PORTE MAILLOT
St Ferdinand
TERNES
Av. de Monceau
de Messine
Av.
St Augus

Boul. Maillot
Av. de la Grande Armée
Mac Mahon
St Joseph
Av. Carnot
Av. Hoche
Courcelles
ST AUGUST

BOIS DE
Bd. de l'Amiral Bruix
Avenue Malakoff
ARGENTINE
Place Charles
Av. de Friedland
Rue
Musée Jaquemart

Allée de Longchamp
CH. DE GAULLE ÉTOILE
Arc de Triomphe de Gaulle
Lido
R. du Faubourg
St Phillipe du Roulé
MIROMESNIL

BOULOGNE
Foch
Avenue
Avenue
Office de Tourisme
GEORGE V
ST. PH. DU ROULÉ
Th. de l Madelein

Place du Mal de Lattre de Tassigny
P.TE DAUPHINE
Hugo
Av.
Rue de
Pontieu
R. Faub St.-Hono

Université Paris IX
Victor
VICTOR HUGO
Kléber
Av. Marceau
des
FRANKLIN ROOSEVELT
Rue
Pontieu
Th. Marigny
Espace Cardin

Boulevard Lannes
BOISSIÈRE
St Pierre de Chaillot
Avenue George-V
Avenue Franklin
Théâtre du Rond-Point
Champs
Élysées
Pla

Avenue
Raymond Poincaré
Musée Guimet
IÉNA
Av. d'Iéna
Pl. Pierre de Serbie
Chap. Grecque
Palais de la Découverte
CHAMPS ELYSÉES
Petit Palais
Élysées
de
Obélisque

Place de Mexico
Aquarium
Av. du Prest
A. MARCEAU
Av. Montaigne
Roosevelt
Grand Palais
Conc

Av. Henri Martin
Av. G. Mandel
Pl. du TROCADÉRO Trocadéro
Musée d'Art Moderne
Av. de New York
Seine
Pont des Invalides
Pont Alexandre III
Pont de la Con
ASSEM
NATION.

RUE DE LA POMPE
Palais de Chaillot
Quai d'Orsay
Palais Bourbon
INVALIDES

Av. Paul Doumer
P.TE d'Iéna
Av. de la Bourdonnais
Rue de l'Université
St Pierre du Gros Caillou
Rue de l'Université
Bou

LA MUETTE
Place de Costa Rica
PASSY
Av. Gustave Eiffel
Avenue Bosquet
Pl. des Invalides
Ste Clotilde

Av. Mozart
Rue de Passy
Quai Branly
Tour Eiffel
PARC DU CHAMP
LA TOUR MAUBOURG
Rue de Grene

R. du Ranelach
Av. du Président Kennedy
Pont de Bir Hakeim
BIR HAKEIM
DE MARS
Av. de Suffren
ÉCOLE MILITAIRE
Hôtel des Invalides
Bd. des Invalides
Varneau

Maison Radio-France
Boulevard
Av. de la Motte
Av. de Tourville
ST F.
XAVIER
Rue de Babylc

Seine
St Léon
Av. de Lowendal
Av. Duquesne
St Francois Xavier
Rue

Pl. Clement Ader
Pont de Grenelle
DUPLEIX
de Grenelle
Avenue de Breteuil
Invalides

Statue de la Liberté
Av. de Suffren
Unesco
Bd. Garibaldi

SÈVRES LECOURBE
Rue de Sèvres

Translation of some French terms in map

French:	English:	French:	English:
Aéroport	Airport	Île	Island
Bibliothèque	Library	Ministère	Ministry
Bourse	Stock exchange	Monastère	Monastery
Bureau de poste	Post office	Monument	Monument
Cave	Cellar	Musée	Museum
Chapelle	Chapel	N-D (Notre-Dame)	Our Lady
Château, Palais	Palace	Parc, Jardin, Champ	Park, Garden
Château-fort-, Fort	Castle, Fort	Piscine	Swimming pool
Cimitière	Cemetery	Place	Square
Cité, Vieille ville	Ancient city	Pont	Bridge
École	School	Porte, Arc	Portal, Arch
Église	Church	Quai	Quay
Gare	Station	Puits, Fontaine	Spring, Fontain
Gare centrale d'Autobus	Bus terminal	Théâtre	Theatre
Hôpital	Hospital	Tour	Tower
Hôtel de ville	Town hall	Université	University

PASTEUR
Rue Lecourbe
Boulevard Pasteur
Musée Bourdelle

St Jean Baptiste de la Salle
Rue de Vaugirard
Bd. Vaugirard

Inst. Pasteur
Gare Montparnasse

From Mud Huts to Palaces

Long ago, Paris was a simple village of mud huts nestled on an island in the river Seine. At the far reaches of the Roman Empire, the city Lutetia, as the Romans called it, was a mere outpost until Julian built a palace for himself in AD358. Barbarians, Parisii boatmen, and Romans fought frequently on the surrounding plain and all left their mark on the developing character of the Parisians.

Attila the Hun was an unwelcome visitor in the 5th century. The legend of St Geneviève, the patron saint of Paris, was created when she 'saved' the city from his horde. A mere 19-year-old, she assured the citizens that the Huns would spare the city, and when her forecast proved correct, a cult formed around her.

Clovis I brought his Frankish armies to Gaul shortly thereafter, defeating the Gallo-Romans at Soissons. He consolidated his power by beating the Alemanni tribe at Tolbiac in 496 and the Visigoths near Poitiers in 507. Clovis moved the capital to Paris and the Merovingian dynasty was underway. He built the Church of the Apostles to honour the remains

Clovis I

Culture

City Symbol

of St Geneviève and was buried there himself. Now the Panthéon sits on the hill, the final resting place for distinguished citizens such as Victor Hugo and Rousseau.

The Capetian dynasty, which began in 987 with Hugues Capet and finally fizzled out 806 years later with the execution of Louis XVI, ruled during a period of growth. The city was improved with public fountains, paved streets, and armed police to maintain order. Paris was emerging as a major European city. All over the country religious fervour inspired the building of some of France's most famous monuments such as Normandy's Mont-St-Michel.

Trade continued to boom throughout the 12th century. Merchants united in powerful guilds, controlling city finance and administration. King Philippe Auguste built a big covered market (Les Halles), improved the waterfront for trade and erected a great wall around the city, protecting it and giving it an urban identity.

The Church remained strong during the difficult Dark Ages and with prosperity grew stronger. In addition to Notre Dame, smaller churches arose in its Gothic likeness, and old Romanesque edifices were restored and rebuilt.

Already a commercial and ecclesiastical centre, Paris also became the centre of scholarship in medieval Europe, and was the first of the great capitals to have a university. A meeting place for scholars and theologians, controversy and debate became part of the city's character, and remain so today.

The upstart scholar Pierre Abelard was the first to attract students to the Left Bank, where the universities of Paris and of the Sorbonne would open (the latter named after Robert de Sorbon). Latin, used in lectures and debates, gave the neighbourhood the name it now bears, *Le Quartier Latin*, still today the city's student centre. The unfortunate Abelard, however, took attracting students too far, and was castrated and sent to a monastery for showing rather too much affection for one, Héloïse.

A City Shaped

In the 14th century, local clothmaker Etienne Marcel led a revolt against the Valois regent, forming an alliance with English forces which in the end led to his losing the support of the majority of his followers. He was assassinated shortly afterwards. All through the Hundred Years' War, control of Paris bounced back and forth between English and French forces. When Joan of Arc laid siege to the city in 1429, Parisians sided with the occupying English and put up stiff resistance. Things finally settled down once Joan of Arc had succeeded in putting Charles VII on the throne.

Joan of Arc

The period of artistic rebirth that followed under François I continued until religious crisis provoked the St Bartholomew Massacre. Thousands of Protestants were killed, but Henri, king of the southwestern realm of Navarre, escaped, and soon became Henri IV, one of France's most celebrated kings.

Henri is known to have switched his religion from Catholic to Protestant and back at least six times, with apparently no qualms at all. The most memorable occasion was upon his triumphant conquest of Paris. He chose that moment to convert to Catholicism, in order to please the powerful Church fathers of Paris as well as the general population. 'Paris,' he said, 'is well worth a mass.'

Thus began the Bourbon monarchy, France's last. The family lavished plenty of money on the city of Paris, trying to keep the unpredictable citizens, the powerful guilds and the Church content. Louis XIV built hospitals and factories, paved new streets and equipped the city with lanterns. Nonetheless, he preferred to move to his luxurious palace at Versailles, where he was in less danger than in the gloomy old Louvre, surrounded as it was by narrow alleys crowded with houses right up to the palace walls. That was altogether too close to the common people.

The new court was moved wholesale out to Versailles, where the splendour of the architecture and the rigidity of court etiquette imposed by Louis reduced the nobility to mere courtiers whose most important responsibility might be to hand the king his undershirt at the *Levée du Roi* ('kingrise' as opposed to sunrise). Five hundred cooks prepared Louis' food, and he commanded 4,000 servants.

In the period leading towards the French Revolution, life in Paris took on two distinct forms. On the one hand, wealthy aristocrats and the burgeoning *bourgeoisie* enjoyed sumptuous decadence, carried on intricate social ceremonies and whirled through the restaurants and theatres of Paris. On the bleaker side, most of the population lived in growing misery, while government debts piled up and up. A bad harvest in 1788 increased the price of bread and revolution fermented as a result.

The storming of the Bastille prison, on 14 July 1789, has long been the symbol of the violent Revolution that shook all of France. As it was the centre of Revolutionary activities and government, as well as the showcase for the notorious guillotine, Paris was, after the Revolution, unassailably confirmed as the capital of power. 'Paris goes her own way,' wrote Victor Hugo, 'and France, irritated, is forced to follow.' In fact it has been said several times since that Paris has almost become a mini-state in its own right, a massive urban area in an essentially rural country.

The Making of Modern Paris

Through the First Empire, the Restoration, and the Second Republic, Paris continued to solidify its position as the

The Coronation of Napoleon Bonaparte

centre of government, arts, fashion and trade, and was regarded as one of Europe's finest capitals, despite its sordid slums and the fundamentally squalid living conditions of the lower classes.

Under the Second Empire (1852–1870) Paris underwent the transformation into the modern city of today. Napoleon III (nephew of Bonaparte) worked with Baron Haussmann, the Prefect of Paris, to carry out extensive urban renewal. Train tracks were set out in all directions, water mains and a sewerage system were installed, great boulevards and avenues were systematically laid out. Slums were razed and the poorest of the poor were displaced outside the city into the eastern suburbs.

The last great struggle between the Parisian population and the wealthy *bourgeoisie* took place after the fall of the Empire under the Third Republic. Hostile to the notion of Prussian occupation following the defeat of Napoleon Bonaparte's army and the Republic's capitulation, the citizens withstood a long siege. When the popular National Guard was ordered to disarm, the *Commune de Paris* was proclaimed at the Hôtel de Ville (town hall).

From the Montmartre hilltop came the call to arms, as workers and revolutionaries united in the struggle for better representation in government. The bloody repression was carried out not by the Prussians, but by regular French troops: 25,000 *communards* died fighting or were executed. This bitter and tragic ending is still a sore spot in the Parisian heart, especially in Montmartre, home to

Providing good service

many of the revolutionaries and anarchists who led the battle. Many of the traditional songs heard in cabarets there still recall the *Commune de Paris*.

Paris in the 20th Century

The turn of the century is often referred to as *La Belle Epoque*, a period of gaiety and artistic renewal. The Eiffel Tower rose unbelievably high and the Metro tunnelled below the city. Between 1880 and 1940, Paris was home to more artists than any other city in the world, both foreign and French, including Picasso, Debussy, Zola, ballet dancer and impressario Diaghilev, and singer Edith Piaf.

In World War I the city was saved heroically when General Gallieni rushed troops to a counter-offensive in the Marne River valley using all available means. Every taxi in town was requisitioned to carry soldiers to the front.

During World War II, Paris was not so lucky, and suffered Ger-

Celebrating the liberation of Paris at the end of World War II

man occupation for four long and dreary years. The city was not destroyed, however, although charges of dynamite had been placed strategically under monuments. In fact, the German Commander Von Cholitz had orders to blow the city up if the Allies arrived, but he wisely chose to surrender instead. Under General de Gaulle's leadership, the Resistance grew steadily throughout the war, and the troops of the Free French were instrumental in the North African and other campaigns. Less memorable in retrospect was the role of the autonomous region of Vichy France, led by World War I general Marshal Pétain. Collaboration with the Nazis was the policy in this region, even though that policy had harrowing implications for the Jewish population in particular. In the end, 25 August 1944 was one of the craziest and happiest days in the city's history, partly because General Eisenhower diplomatically allowed the French troops, under the leadership of General Leclerc, to be the first to enter Paris.

After the rationing, death and horrors of war, Paris prospered in the 1950s and early 60s. Bebop, Rock and Roll and tourists travelled across the Atlantic. In May 1968, the city saw its most important upheaval since the Commune. Opponents to the Algerian War, disenchanted students and trade unions struck together and paralysed Paris. Charles de Gaulle himself fled the city, just as kings and emperors had done before him, fearful of the

De Gaulle became unpopular

wrath of its citizens. He relinquished power to his former prime minister Georges Pompidou.

In 1977, reform made it possible for Parisians to elect a mayor for the first time. Jacques Chirac has since presided over the City Council at the Hôtel de Ville. In addition, each *arrondissement* elects its own mayor, and the administration of many city affairs is delegated out to separate town halls. In 1989 France celebrated the bicentennial of the French Revolution, an event which led to an orgy of self-congratulation, and major celebrations in Paris. The Eiffel Tower in particular had a complete overhaul.

Since 1981, the President has been François Mitterrand, elected for two seven-year terms. As President, he has implemented a vast plan of public works in the city. Like Napoleon III, he will certainly leave his signature on the capital.

Tour de Paris

Among the great projects that mark the Mitterrand decade are: the improvement of the Louvre Museum with the construction of the Pyramid, the Opéra at La Bastille, the new Finance Ministry at Bercy, the Grande Arche at La Défense, the La Villette Museum and Science Park, the Arab World Institute opposite Notre Dame, the Quai d'Orsay Museum, many extensive new road and tunnel systems to ease traffic, the development of outlying areas, and improved public transport. Side by side with the works of Philippe Auguste and Baron Haussmann, these achievements create new harmony in the city.

The spirit of the city today is still a mixture of fractious Gaulish rebellion and refined Roman arts, spiced with the exotic contributions of immigrants from Africa and Asia. A mad poet in Montmartre, a fashion model in diamonds at the Dior boutique, an African student on the Left Bank, an early-rising baker kneading *croissants*: Paris is home to all. Its streets are living theatres, so walk them and observe.

Historical Highlights

52BC: *Lutetia* founded by the Romans and occupied by the Parisii.

AD300: Germanic invasions by the Alemanni tribe. The city settles on the Ile de la Cité and takes the name of Paris.

451: Paris repels the Huns with the help of St Geneviève, who becomes the focal point of a cult.

6th century: The Frankish people settle in Paris.

987: The Capetian dynasty begins, bringing years of prosperity.

12th century: Trade booms. The cathedral of Notre Dame is built on the Ile de la Cité. Philippe Auguste orders the construction of a great wall around the city.

13th century: The Universities of Paris and the Sorbonne created.

1356-8: Revolt led by cloth-maker Etienne Marcel against the incompetent Valois dynasty. Marcel was assassinated after making an alliance with the hated English.

1572: Fervent religious debate leads to the St Bartholomew massacre, in which thousands of Protestants died.

1594: Henri IV takes Paris.

1682: Louis XIV moves into Versailles palace and turns the nobility into mere courtiers.

1789: The storming and capture of the Bastille prison heralds the beginning of the French Revolution.

1793: Execution of Louis XVI.

1804-48: The first Empire, under Napoleon Bonaparte is declared, and is then followed by the Restoration of the (constitutional) Monarchy.

1848: Revolution in Paris, the Second Republic declared.

1860: The number of *arrondise-ments*, or districts, rises from only 12 to 20. Today's smart 16th has its designation changed from the unlucky 13th.

1853-70: Under the Second Empire and Napoleon III, nephew of Bonaparte, Baron Haussmann gives Paris its present shape and appearance, particularly notable for its grand boulevards.

1870-1: Paris under seige by the Prussian Army.

1871: The *Commune de Paris* civil rebellion ends in bloodshed. Many of the rebels are executed in the Père Lachaise cemetery.

1889: The World Fair provokes the construction of several key monuments, especially the Eiffel Tower.

1940-4: German Occupation of Paris lasts for four years. Liberation comes on 25 August 1944, one of the happiest days in Parisian history.

1968: General strike (led by the student population) paralyses the city. Street fighting and massive demonstrations. General de Gaulle, now very unpopular, eventually hands over power to Georges Pompidou.

1977: Death of Pompidou.

1977: Elections for mayor of the city are held for the first time, Jacques Chirac becomes the first incumbent of the Hôtel de Ville (town hall).

1981: François Mitterrand, President of the Republic, initiates a major plan for renewing the city including Le Grand Louvre, the Opéra at Bastille, the Grande Arche of La Défense, etc.

1989: Celebrations in honour of the Bicentennial of the French Revolution, and 100th birthday of the Eiffel Tower.

Day Itineraries

DAY 1

Notre Dame and the Left Bank

Begin this full day in Paris where the city itself first started, Ile de la Cité, on an island in the middle of the river Seine. Visit the Gothic cathedral of Notre Dame. From there, wind through the mosaic of streets on the Left (south) Bank. Discover the Latin Quarter, a student hang-out since Roman times, with its mix of scholarship and entertainment. To the Luxembourg Gardens, the park most loved by Parisians, and from there to the city's tallest office building, La Tour Montparnasse, in time for sunset.

Begin early in the morning and wear your most comfortable shoes. This walking tour takes you from the centre of the city towards its

Sainte Chapelle, within the Conciergerie

southern end, with plenty of places to stop and rest your feet. So travel at your leisure; you can always hop on the Metro to speed to the next destination, particularly towards the end of the day.

The **Ile de la Cité** (Metro: Cité), one of two islands in the Seine, site of the earliest primitive city and later the Roman administrative centre, is the main office of the French police and the Court of Justice, all in the grand **Conciergerie**. This imposing château stands on the foundations of the city's first royal dwelling. Later it held prisoners during the French Revolution, including Queen Marie Antoinette.

In this pompous setting is a diamond, the **Sainte Chapelle**, with a tall and sharp silhouette which is very visible in the overall complex. This narrow and vaulted Gothic chapel (follow the sign inside the main entrance on the Cour du Mai) was built by Saint Louis, King of France, in 1264. The proliferation of deep-coloured glass windows in scalloped stonework and the excellent restoration of the walls and columns lend the building a delicate beauty. Chamber music lovers should note the bulletin board with concert schedules. The chapel is open daily from 10am, but is sometimes inaccessible when notorious bandits are on trial in the court-rooms next door.

The Conciergerie

Turn back and head towards the (presently invisible) Notre Dame, via the pedestrian **Place Lepine**, for the daily flower and bird market. Flower sellers are here from 9am–7pm daily, except Sunday, when birds are the speciality.

Now walk round the corner to

21

Gargoyle on Notre Dame

the **Parvis de Notre Dame**, a cobbled square in front of the great cathedral (open 8am–6.45pm).

Notre Dame's stone foundation was laid in 1163 but it was only completed about 200 years later. The scene of various dramas in French history, from medieval justice (executions were carried out here) to the coronation of an Emperor (Napoleon I), the cathedral's ancient walls are steeped in history, reflected in the innumerable faces and figures carved upon them. The three portals (main doorways) to the cathedral are typical examples of Gothic religious art, each a 'book' for the illiterate of the Middle Ages, recounting the stories of the Bible and the lives of saints. Inside, 29 separate chapels line the nave, transept and choir. The **Rose Windows**, 31ft (9 metres) in diameter, have been extensively restored but parts of them still date from the 13th century.

The carved wooden choir stalls are early 17th century, and the **Pietà Statue** decorating the large altar at the far end of the cathedral was commissioned by Louis XIII during the same period, an offering in thanks for the birth of his son and heir to the throne, who eventually completed the memorial. In veneration on either side of the fallen Christ and his earthly mother are statues of the regal father and son.

The **Trésor** (closed on Sunday and religious holidays), also in the rear of the church, is the cathedral's museum, displaying religious artifacts, richly embroidered robes and jewelled chalices.

As you leave the church, you will see signs to the **Bell Tower**, and if you are up to a 270-ft (82-metre) spiraling ascent, you can visit the huge brass bell and come eye-to-eye with the devilish gargoyles who contemplate the city from their privileged perch.

Leave the cathedral, walk around it to the right, go through the little park and to the end of the island. There you will find an unusual and starkly moving monument in memory of World War II deportees **(Monument de la Déportation)** set down into the ground. Descend into the pit through narrow passages between thick, rough walls, and come face to face with the black metal bars. There is a feeling of desolation. Yet at the same time, the monument is strangely calm: a sheltered, windless sun-trap inviting rest and reflection.

From there, take the Pont St Louis to the next island, the placid **Ile St Louis**. The attractions of this 'island of calm' in the storm of the city are the shady riverfront, the fashionable art galleries and tea rooms, and at 31 Rue St Louis en I'Ile (just at the other end of the bridge from Ile de la Cité), **Maison Berthillon**, where you can sample what is often called the best ice-cream in Paris while sitting out in the sun.

Afterwards backtrack across Ile de la Cité and cross the Seine to the Left Bank, where a walk along the *quai* affords a fine view of Notre Dame and its flying buttresses, as well as an opportunity to browse at the characteristic green bookstalls, which also sell quantities of postcards, prints and maps. There are some collector's items to be ferreted out here.

More books, in English mostly, are in store at the historic **Shakespeare and Co.** in Rue de la Bûcherie, just off the left of the tiny Square Viviani (Metro: St Michel). Fans of James Joyce will know that Paris was his second home and that bookshop-owner Sylvia Beach was his banker and publisher of his once-scandalous

Notre Dame seen from the south

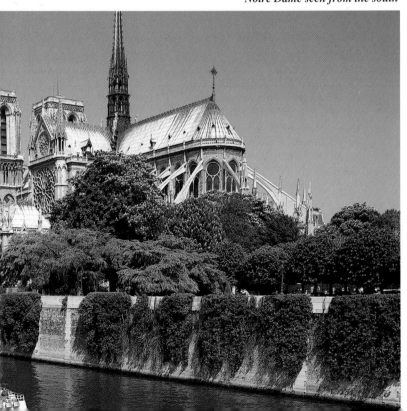

novel, *Ulysses*. The spirit of famous and would-be expatriate writers haunts the shop, which is well worth exploring.

Head south into the narrow lanes. Now you are smack in the centre of the **Latin Quarter**, one of the busiest parts of town and favoured by students, shoppers and good-time seekers. These narrow ways, redolent in the evening with Greek and Middle Eastern cooking and busy with strolling entertainers, recall much older times, despite the electric lights and modern fashions. Street performers set up here as they have for centuries, and pass a hat among the crowd. Through the occasional kitchen door left ajar you may see a chef spooning up steaming heaps of Algerian *couscous*. But although this is a popular quarter for good value dining out, it is not the place for the best cuisine of Paris. Revolving spits of lamb are roasting in the windows of sandwich shops; a long sharp knife cuts the thin slices off into an open pitta bread.

At the minuscule **Théâtre de la Huchette**, the troupe has been playing *The Bald Soprano* for over 50 years. Tickets are available. Amble down the pedestrian streets of La Huchette and La Harpe up to **Boulevard St Michel**. Walk up to the crossroads with **Boulevard St Germain**, where the two big roads meet and thereby set the limits of the famous Latin Quarter.

Books on the Boulevard St Michel

On the far corner here stands the **Cluny Museum**, the city's only surviving Gothic residence, next to the ruins of a Roman bath house, a second-century vestige. This is really one of the best museums in a city which boasts some of the world's finest. The building lends itself perfectly to the display of furnishings, fabrics, stained glass, architectural ornaments and religious reliquaries from the Middle Ages. Upstairs, the Cluny's prize is the series of tapestries known as *The Lady and the Unicorn*, a 15th-century marvel depicting the five senses as well as a sixth, mysterious and unexplained one to be left to your imagination.

After much medieval food for thought, you will be thinking of some more terrestrial fare, and you will find plenty of choice for lunch up the Blvd St Germain at the crossroads called **Odéon** (Metro: Odéon). I would recommend

In the Cluny Museum

A legend in St Germain des Prés

the **Chope d'Alsace**, at 4 Carrefour de l'Odéon, which will satisfy the heartiest of appetites with typical food from the east of France (especially *choucroute* – sauerkraut with a selection of pork cuts and sausages), grilled meat and seafood. The list of daily specials, often as long as the regular menu, is based on the chef's mood and the morning's market. Prices (count on about 180 Francs per person) are fair for the quality and quantity served, and the wine list is tempting.

Thus revived, your next step is to continue up Boulevard St Michel towards **St Germain des Prés**. Along the way, you pass Rue de Buci on the right and Rue Mabillon on the left, both leading to colourful markets. There are shops for every kind of clothes all along the way, from the classic Marcel Fuks for men to the wacky, unisex Atomic City and the voguish Comme Ça des Halles for women on the cusp of fashion.

The church of **St Germain des Prés**, (Metro: St Germain des Prés) though one of the city's oldest (built in the 11th and 12th centuries, Romanesque in style) is not one of the loveliest. The square is better known for the cafés **Flore** and **Deux Magots** and the **Brasserie Lipp**, hangouts for the literati since Jean-Paul Sartre and Simone de Beauvoir held court here.

Turn down Rue Bonaparte, away from the church and towards Montparnasse, to find another stylish row of shops – even Yves St Laurent is here, with a shop on the pleasant **Place Saint Sulpice**

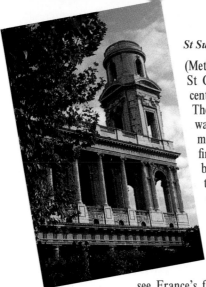

St Sulpice, where Victor Hugo got married

(Metro: St Sulpice). Less animated than St Germain, this square and its 19th-century fountain have a dignified charm. The church, where author Victor Hugo was married, is welcoming despite its monumental proportions; there is a fine old pipe organ inside (check the bulletin board for scheduled concerts); the first chapel on the right (Chapelle de Sainte Agnès) was decorated by Eugène Delacroix, one of the greatest painters of the Romantic period. As you leave the St Sulpice, look up to the building on the other side of the square – you may see France's favourite actress Catherine Deneuve leaning out of her window!

As afternoon wends its way to evening, just a short walk down Rue Henry de Jouvenel (immediately left out of the church) and Rue Ferou brings you to the **Jardin du Luxembourg**. Enter by the **Petit Luxembourg Museum**, which has changing exhibitions, and reach the central pond by way of the **Palais du Luxembourg**, once a royal palace and today seat of the French Senate. If you retreat to the far end of the gardens and look over the top of the palace, you should be able to see Sacré Coeur on the Montmartre hilltop, like a fat white pigeon roosting above the city.

Take a break in the sunshine under the shade of the chestnut trees. This park is much more of a recreation area than the Tuileries, and a particular favourite with many Parisians because of its elegance and its central location. But don't tarry after dark, or you'll find yourself camping out for the night behind high locked

Parisians enjoy the Jardin du Luxembourg

gates, which are closed at nightfall by bell-ringing guardians.

Leave the park by the west exit (level with the round pond) onto Rue de Fleurus, where Gertrude Stein and her life-long companion Alice B Toklas lived and reigned over artistic society and the 'Lost Generation' at No 27. Their *coterie* included Hemingway, Picasso, Ford Madox Ford, Cézanne, Matisse and other artists in that period from 1907 to Stein's death in 1946. Although these luminaries are gone from the street now, you might see Joan Baez, if she happens to be staying in her house there.

Continue some way down Fleurus before turning right on Notre Dame des Champs (Metro: St Placide) to reach Rue de Rennes. From there you can walk straight down to Montparnasse (or take the Metro) to arrive at the big black **Tour Montparnasse**.

To get a view over the territory you've covered, take the superfast elevator (9.30am to 11pm, admission fee), to the 56th-floor terrace and rooftop. At this height, the traffic below is seen but not heard; and wide avenues ribboned in green trees stretch away below the rooftops with their characteristic red chimney pots. The glassed-in bar provides signs with information on what you are seeing from each point of reference. But the helicopter pad on the very top (59 floors up) is more exciting; open to the wind and seemingly unbounded on the sides, there is a slight thrill of danger (but no real danger in fact) – perhaps this is why there are not usually too many people up here! To see where you've been, look due north and you should spot the green sward of the Luxembourg gardens, and further in the distance, the two solid square towers of Notre Dame.

For dinner

At dusk, the sun sets beyond the Eiffel Tower. On a good clear evening, Montparnasse is the best place to watch the natural fireworks at the end of day, and the sparkles of artificial light blooming one by one across the city landscape.

Back on the street, you can head for dinner at one of Hemingway's favourites: **La Closerie des Lilas** (171 Blvd Montparnasse) or **La Coupole** (102 on the same street). The first is rather special; it has a subdued atmosphere and a piano bar and is more expensive as well as being some way down the boulevard. The second is a large and noisy place to dance, eat, see and be seen. Both have plenty of variety on the menu; for a complete meal with wine, count on at least 200 Francs per person, but you can do it for less. They're open late, as are many of the local restaurants, cafés and bars, and there are plenty of taxis to take you back to your hotel.

The Grand Boulevards

Today's itinerary begins with a panoramic view of Paris from the Arc de Triomphe. This is the Paris of the grand and sweeping avenues, created by Baron Haussmann. Start by walking down the Champs Elysées to Place de la Concorde and the Tuileries; side-step the Louvre to the Palais Royal and on to the redeveloped Halles and the Georges Pompidou Centre.

Up the Champs Elysées

The first half of this day is spent walking the long straight line known as the **Triumphal Way**. A major feature of Paris, it is not very intimate, and perhaps no longer the most spectacular, even though it has been extended right out to the new Grande Arche at La Défense. The Champs Elysées is still the most famous part of this route. (A hint for those with tired feet: ride down the avenue in green bus No 73 and save some energy for later).

A familiar monument, the grand **Arc de Triomphe** (Metro: Charles de Gaulle-Etoile) straddles a hectic cobbled traffic circle. Construction began in 1806, but it wasn't completed until 30 years later, all in commemoration of the victories of Napoleon Bonaparte. In 1920, the arch became the site for the **Tomb of the Unknown Soldier**; a Flame of Remembrance was lit.

It was the 'other'

Napoleon (nephew of the Corsican original, known to some as 'Napoleon the Little') who ordered the city planning that gave the **Place de l'Etoile** ('of the star') its name. With the Prefect of Paris, Baron Haussmann, he created the city's wide boulevards flanked by chestnut trees, including the 12 avenues that radiate out from the Arc de Triomphe. Partly motivated by the need to control rebellious crowds (hence the wide, straight thoroughfares), the two of them created an architectural legend, and greatly advanced the art of urban planning.

You can take an elevator to the top of the Arc de Triomphe (9am to 6pm every day). The view is still largely the same as it was once Haussmann had finished with the city, and includes the spacious **Bois de Boulogne** forest to the west and of course the **Avenue des Champs Elysées** just at your·feet.

One hundred years ago, this glitzy strip was little more than a bridlepath, suitable for closed carriage rides and intimate suppers in discreet restaurants. Luxurious private homes later gave way to sumptuous hotels, expensive shops and desirable corporate addresses. Now, the avenue sparkles at night, but not with the diamonds and bright personalities of its heyday; heavy traffic and neon lights are its principal jewels.

Cinemas, cafés and fast food places provide most of the

entertainment today; the shops and restaurants are generally overpriced and aimed at tourists; and the people walking up and down the avenue are mostly foreigners or teenagers from the suburbs who come in for hamburgers and a film.

Despite the fading reputation, it is still fun to stroll down the wide pavements of the Champs Elysées and look at people. The top end is dominated by airline offices and the **Tourist Office**, on the south side. On the same side half way down is the **Hotel George V** (on the avenue of the same name, Metro: George V), which is beautifully decorated with a fine restaurant and garden terrace.

The sheer size of the Champs Elysées is emphasized even more by some of the stores such as the **Hippo Citroen** or the **Pub Renault**, where you can check out the latest car models and the Renault Museum over a thick steak or a beer, and the **Virgin Megastore**, a truly mega book and record shop which recently challenged Sunday trading laws. At the bottom of the slope, where the avenue opens

Hotel George V

out, you will find **Le Drugstore**, which has outlived its fashionableness, but still draws a crowd to its American-style restaurant.

At this point the avenue becomes far more attractive in summer, with its serene fountains and shady park, with several interesting theatres. To the right just down Avenue Franklin Roosevelt is the **Rond Point (Théâtre Renaud-Barrault),** which was created by two of France's finest actors, who also happen to be living one of the longest-running love stories ever. You can walk in for a look at the fun décor, or stop for a drink in the bar. The restaurant **Laserre** (tel: 43 595343) is a little further down this avenue on the right, opposite the Palais de la Découverte. This discreet building is one of the top ten restaurants in town – for both cuisine and price! Count on 500 Francs per person, but the choice of wine from the outstanding cellar may make that substantially higher.

Back in the parkland on the left of the Champs Elysées, the **Espace Cardin** (half-way to Place de la Concorde) is another prestigious performance space, where a garden restaurant features a buffet lunch. If you're intimidated by eating with celebrities, avoid this one!

The **Place de la Concorde**, and its commanding, 33-centuries-old obelisk from the tomb of Ramses III in Egypt, is another city landmark. Eighty-five thousand square yards (70,833sq m) of cobblestone and traffic cacophony, the Place seems just as crowded

Fountain, Place de la Concorde

as it must have been when Louis XVI was beheaded there, and the drivers are almost as aggressive as a crowd at an execution.

Dash across the traffic into the relative peace of the **Jardin des Tuileries**, the long narrow gardens leading to the Louvre. The central alley forms part of the long straight line drawn directly from the Arc de Triomphe. Here too, Haussmann went to work tearing down the remains of part of a castle, opening up the streets along the wall. The sunny pools and patches of green lawn alternate with shaded alleys where you'll find outdoor cafés, a children's play area, and finally, almost inside the encircling arms of the Palais du Louvre, the **Arc de Triomphe du Carrousel**, a miniature mirror-image of the Arc de Triomphe which marks the end of the lengthy Triumphal Way.

At this stage, if you can't resist the temptation of the Louvre, turn to itinerary 6: *The New Louvre*. But I suggest you leave the Louvre till later, and meanwhile leave the Tuileries behind to dash across the busy **Rue de Rivoli**. Walk through the arcades past the gilded statue of Joan of Arc to the Place du Palais Royal (Metro: Palais Royal). The adjacent Place Colette is home to the **Comédie Française**, the famous classical theatre founded by Molière. Follow the arcades to the entrance of the **Palais Royal Gardens**. About 200 years ago, the *Palais* really was a royal palace, until Philippe d'Orléans, who was living there, sank deep into debt. He added arcades and rented boutique space to solve his cash-flow problem. It became a very popular speakers' corner and played an important role in the Revolution.

Today the shops are still there, beyond the square of black and white columns designed by Burennes, which are matched by the window shades of the surrounding buildings. Most of the shops offer antiques and collector's items, especially coins and military

Between the Champs Elysées and the Tuileries

Galerie Colbert

decorations. These dim little boutiques are full of uncommon treasures for those who know how to value them.

Part of the Palais is now occupied by the Ministry of Culture; other apartments are still in private hands. It is said that these apartments are beyond price – families hang on to them forever. It is easy to see why: they are centrally located yet quiet, soothing to the eye and spirit. Sometimes you can glimpse a high-ceilinged room behind a heavy brocade curtain. Even the children running through the park have something of another era about them, as they roll their hoops along the sandy paths.

Slip out the far end of the rectangular gardens; cross over the tiny Rue des Petits Champs. To your left are the **Galerie Vivienne** and the **Galerie Colbert**, recently restored skylit passages with mosaic walkways, leading to Rue Vivienne and the French National Library, not far from the Opéra. To your right is the **Place des Victoires**, a charming circle which was originally built to display the statue of Louis XIV in the centre. Now fashion is king both in the Place and the narrow streets radiating out from it. The designers' boutiques are New Age outposts in the regal architecture.

Here you are just around the corner (past the main post office on Rue du Louvre) from the restaurant **Au Pied de Cochon**, one of the best-known in Paris, in a row of restaurants on Rue Coquillière. As a carry-over from older times, when market deliveries were made in the wee hours before stalls opened up, it is open day and night. One of the favourite dishes of the hard-working market hands was the thick and cheesy onion soup, still on the menu. For a complete meal, you should count on 250 Francs per person.

You are now on the fringes of **Les Halles**, visible here as a covered-

Les Halles and St Eustache

in parkland with escalators down to the shopping centre. The name refers to the city food market which clogged up the neighbourhood streets from the 12th century until 1969, when it was demolished in the name of safety and urban renewal. Now a more ordinary commerce takes place in about 200 boutiques of every sort inside the multi-level shopping centre (Metro: Les Halles).

But don't go down the escalators – unless you really want to go shopping. Instead, have a quick look inside the rather sombre and grand **St Eustache** to your left before walking around the edge of the parkland by way of Rue Berger to the lively **Place des Innocents**, where there's usually a good crowd gathered around the fountain. There is a permanent fashion parade of the wackiest looks in this square. Those who knew it before renewal deplore the high-priced boutiques that have replaced all of the good old places, but it must be admitted that it is as animated and attractive as ever. The **Café Costes** is a favourite meeting place, with its distinctive designer décor.

At the corner of Rue Berger and **Rue St Denis**, take a good look up and down the latter. This is the beginning of the city's red light street. The hard core is several blocks down to the left, and not very picturesque. Where you are now, there are plenty of sex shops, but also plenty of cheap eateries and interesting shops and a few nicer places (**The Front Page**, with American specialities like spare ribs and chilli and an American-style bar).

All the comings and goings in the pedestrian areas, the variety of commerce and nightlife help Les Halles retain something of its former dynamism from the days when it was the city's main market. Drifters, bargain hunters, sensation seekers, local residents and young people mix like a crazy salad. Hang on to your wallet.

Head south from Place des Innocents towards the river to turn left onto Rue des Lombards. Use it to cross Boulevard Sebastopol into the region of Paris known as the Marais. Instantly you are into the Marais' characteristic narrow, winding streets with small shops and bars. Turn left up Rue St Martin to **St Merri**, an ornate medieval church nestled tightly amidst the shops and restaurants. You may hear music floating out of its doors, for there are frequent concerts in the church, particularly at weekends. The church bell has been tolling the hours since 1331 and is the oldest in Paris.

Now you are just around the corner from the most visited attraction (twice the numbers for the Louvre) in the city, the modern museum known affectionately as 'Beaubourg' after the street which runs behind it, which has been looming on your

Street Style, Les Halles

horizon ever since Les Halles. Its official name is the **Georges Pompidou Arts and Cultural Centre** (Metro: Rambuteau, open noon–10pm, Monday to Friday, 10am–10pm Saturday and Sunday), and it acts as a massive magnet for this whole area of Paris, drawing people through the narrow streets to its doors to the tune of eight million visitors a year, or 24,000 per day – of whom 60 percent are French. The museum has become so popular that it is hard to remember the passionate debate about its 'inside-out' architecture (blue units are air-conditioning, green are water circulation, red are transport routes and yellow indicates electric circuits) Comments like 'looks like an oil refinery' are rarely heard today. Although the furnishings definitely show wear and tear, what goes on inside is still as exciting as ever.

While many Paris museums seem to be staid, whispery places, this one is an exception the minute it comes in sight. Fire-eaters, mimes, musicians and an assorted crew of urban nomads have adopted the sloping cobbled terrace. Students love the library and music room. The ride is free on the escalators that snake up the outside of the building in a transparent tube to the fifth-floor rooftop cafeteria and viewing platform. By the south end of the building is a quartz clock counting the seconds to the year 2000. And further south, between Beaubourg and the St Merri church, is a colourful fountain of grotesque creatures mixed with modern inventions spouting water in different directions.

The Pompidou's permanent collection is the **National Museum of Modern Art**, on the fourth floor. There is a more serious art-appreciation atmosphere in these well-lit and comfortable rooms. Paintings and sculptures include works from different periods and schools: Fauvism, Cubism, Futurism and various artists including Matisse, Kandinsky, Mondrian and Dubuffet. These permanent exhibitions are well worth the visit, and generally not too crowded. If you see a long queue, it is probably for a temporary show. Occasionally, they are quite controversial, and you may hear art lovers arguing on the way out.

On the mezzanine level there is

usually a free exhibition or two, often something zany and challenging. It could be, for example, a show of household lamp design, some sample 'sonic environments' to immerse oneself in, or an exhibition of mud and clay architecture.

The **Salle Garance** is for zealous cinephiles, specialising in films that don't often make it to local theatres. For avant garde sounds, there is the IRCAM (Institute of Research and Co-ordination into Acoustics and Music), a prestigious centre directed by Pierre Boulez. The museum also welcomes dance and theatre troupes to its basement stage.

There is a complete posting of all the centre's events and exhibits on the ground floor; some things are free. The information booths stock brochures in many languages, and there is a very good bookshop also on the ground floor.

For dining I suggest **Bouchons** at the top end of Rue des Halles. Here you'll find an elegant atmosphere and good service for its French cuisine, some of it distinctly *nouvelle* (about 140 Francs per person). Downstairs there's a piano bar with a more relaxed tone.

Spoilt for choice

Selection number two is less chic but just as French, **Le Chien Qui Fume** ('the smoking dog'!), in a quiet corner at the top of Rue du Pont Neuf. Shellfish and hearty French cooking at reasonable prices, as well as all-day service from noon until 2am, (costs around 170 Francs per person).

Georges Pompidou Arts and Cultural Centre (Beaubourg)

Marais and Bastille

This itinerary takes you through one of the most distinctive and well-loved areas of Paris: the Marais. The beauty of the buildings lining the narrow, twisted streets can be traced to the 16th and 17th centuries, when well-to-do Parisians built their 'hôtels particuliers' (private residences) here. In this itinerary, south of the Rue St Antoine is not so interesting as north. Therefore, if time is short, go straight from the Hôtel de Ville to St Paul by Metro, then begin at the Hôtel de Sully. The section of the itinerary that goes beyond the Place de Bastille with its shiny new opera house is primarily for those interested in contemporary art and alternative Paris culture. To complete the whole route in a day, choose one or two museums, and content yourself with the windows of most galleries.

You should begin your day at the **Hôtel de Ville** (Metro: Hôtel de Ville). This is the main branch of the local government, and has been the fiefdom of the Mayor of Paris since 1977.

The first Hôtel de Ville was built along the bank of the river Seine during the Renaissance, at the height of the neighbourhood's popularity. It was burned to the ground during the insurrection of the Commune in 1871.

Viollet-le-Duc undertook its reconstruction. This Parisian architect is renowned in France for his restoration and re-creation of medieval edifices. Besides the Hôtel de Ville, he restored Notre Dame and other cathedrals, the castle at Pierre-fonds, and the entire city of Carcassonne in the southwest of France.

Hôtel de Ville

There is a convenient post office in the Hôtel de Ville (on the side with the very pleasant courtyard), and on the Rue de Rivoli there is an entrance to an exhibition area with some information about the town.

You may be tempted to tarry on **Rue de Rivoli**. This is a very busy shopping street, with giants like the BHV department store directly opposite, and other speciality shops selling shoes, clothes, pianos, whatever. From here, to your left the street leads right up past the Louvre and to the Place de la Concorde; to your right it leads into Rue St Antoine and the Marais. Most large international chain stores are

Restaurant in the Marais

represented along its length. But to discover the Marais, you must take quieter paths, and I suggest you begin at the **Saint Gervais Church**, which is in a quiet square on the other (eastern) side of the Hôtel de Ville. The monumental Gothic style of this church is original, not reconstructed. Restoration has been carried out, however, and notably after a German shell exploded here in 1918, killing 51 people at a Holy Friday mass.

Continue up Rue François Miron to the left of the church, contemplating the row of houses from No 4 to 14 built in 1732. Farther along, some distance past half-timbered houses on the left, No 68 is another remarkable residence, the **Hôtel de Beauvais**, dating from 1665. Louis XIV gave it to his mistress, and when she was gone, Mozart lived there briefly.

Turn right into Rue du Jouy and go across the crossroads by the Tribunal and into Rue Charlemagne. Hidden away to the right (signposted) in this quiet residential district is the **Bibliothèque Forney**, open in the afternoons. Before it became the city's historical and fine arts library, this building was known as the Hôtel de Sens, which the Archbishop of Sens began building in 1470. The pointed towers on the corners are a familiar landmark to Parisians. Later, the mansion was inhabited by Marguerite de Valois, first wife of Henri IV, notorious for her penchant for young lovers.

Continue down the rather dull Rue Charlemagne to where it suddenly becomes far more interesting at **Rue St Paul** (Metro: St

Paul). This little street is a favourite of mine, with its exotic boutiques and restaurants. Take it left up to Rue Saint Antoine. This wide avenue leads back into the Rue de Rivoli, but you should cross it and turn right to reach the **Hôtel de Sully**, which now opens its doors to the public as the *Caisse National des Monuments Historiques*. This umbrella organisation offers the best guided tours of Parisian monuments, museums and sites. Inside, you can visit the lovely gardens and the current exhibition, and also pick up an illustrated map of the Marais (open daily from 10am to 6pm).

Now turn back and retrace your steps down Rue St Antoine past the church, take a right on Rue Malher and from there go down the **Rue des Rosiers**. This is the heart of the Jewish Quarter, as one look at the specialised shops and restaurants will tell you. One of the street's best places to eat is **Jo Goldenberg's**. The Goldenberg family is of Russian origin, and their recipes reflect it. Borscht is a favourite starter here, and the stuffed carp is the star of the menu. Prices are moderate but if you go for the caviar it will cost more!

Hôtel de Sully

Another choice would be to eat your way slowly down the street, stopping at stands for falafel and various sandwiches on pitta or rye bread, pickled lemons, smoked sausages and pastries; sampling a mixture of culinary traditions from both Eastern Europe and the Middle East.

At the end of the street, turn right on Rue Vieille du Temple and follow it up some distance to Rue de la Perle. Turn right again to reach the Place Thorigny and the **Picasso Museum**, on the left off a little square. The museum is in the **Hôtel Salé**, so-called because its 17th-century owner grew rich through the lucrative activity of collecting taxes on salt. Oddly, the very modern masterpieces fit superbly into the well-restored decor. The chandeliers, benches and chairs were designed by Picasso's friend Alberto Giacometti.

The paintings and other works were part of the artist's legacy, and are arranged chronologically. There are also a

The Picasso Museum in the Hôtel Salé

Parisiennes both

number of works by other artists which were part of his own collection. The museum opened in 1985, and long queues have been its fate ever since. Even so, it is worth waiting to see so many of this prolific artist's works displayed in one place. It is open from 9.30am to 6pm and is closed on Tuesday.

Continue your walk down Rue de Parc Royal, then right into Rue Payenne and past the two pretty little parks bordering it. This part of the Marais has grown more chic since the museum opened, with a number of trendy boutiques and art galleries. Some of them have set up in butcher's or baker's premises, and kept the original shop fronts. Several other Renaissance *hôtels* are in the midst of restoration.

Stop on the corner of Rue des Francs Bourgeois at **Marais Plus**, a wonderful giftshop and tearoom. The shop has a great collection of the most eccentric teapots (plus a book about them). Refresh yourself with a big piece of freshly baked cake or pie and a pot of fragrant tea.

Just around the corner, a few places to the left on Rue de Sévigné is the **Carnavalet Museum**. This is the city's historical museum, again in a well-restored *hôtel*. Rarely crowded, the displays cover aspects of urban life from the Middle Ages through the French

Revolution, and also show some of the furnishings and souvenirs of Mme de Sévigné, a 17th-century character known for her voluminous correspondence and her virulent gossip. A creaky old place with a quiet little garden, the museum is open every day (except Tuesday) from 10am to 6.40pm.

Walk the rest of the way down the boutique-lined Rue des Francs Bourgeois to the **Place des Vosges**, a highlight of the Marais, and a unique Parisian square. The red brick arcades give it a singular appeal. This is the oldest square in Paris, and its name is in honour of the first French department to pay its taxes to the new Republic.

At the far corner of the square, **Victor Hugo's House** is open to the public at No 6. The author of *Les Misérables* was also expert with a carpenter's tools: some of the

39

In Place des Vosges

furniture is crafted by his own hands. The house is open from 10am to 5.40pm (closed Monday).

The covered walkways of the Place are animated much as they must have been in Hugo's time, with street singers and organ players. Peek in the shop **Mythes et Légendes**, selling antiques, tapestries and oddments from around the world.

Leave the Marais down Rue Birague and Rue St Antoine and turn left for the **Place de la Bastille** (Metro: Bastille).

In the centre of the former site of the notorious prison captured on 14 July 1789, stands the **July Column**. It was erected in the last century to honour the victims of the revolutions of 1830 and 1848. Caught in mid-flight high atop is a golden statue, the *Génie de la Bastille*, a representation of Liberty.

The old Bastille prison has long gone. In its stead a new fortress has just taken shape here, all silver and glass looking very sleek and impenetrable. It is the **Opéra de la Bastille**, one of President François Mitterrand's great projects. Plagued by controversy from the start, and with a multitude of changes in design and administration, the Opéra is still in its infancy. Time will tell if it achieves its goal of making great music more accessible to the population of Paris.

Your destination now is **Rue de la Roquette**, branching off near the Opéra and heading east all the way to the Père Lachaise cemetery. You are now out of both the winding Marais and the grand and uniform Haussmann's Paris, and away from the tourists: this street is not beautiful, and it becomes increasingly run-down. Once the site of a women's prison where public executions were spectator sports, the street has shed its grisly reputation and is now a trendy place to hang out. If you're ready for dinner already, there is some unusual fare and a relaxed atmosphere at No 36 in **Goûts et Couleurs du Monde**, which has changing ethnic menus at moderate prices (about 80 Francs).

Further along, at No 25, another carry-over from the old days is the **Stamp and Coin Shop**, and nearby, a **Model Train Shop**, both havens for collectors. Otherwise, there are several new clothing shops with some original and exotic items in the windows. Some stylish and hippy decorative arts are also available.

Further down, the main draw is still the art galleries. Through the arch at No 57 opposite the Théâtre de la Bastille, take a look at **J et J Donguy**, where two brothers show up-and-coming artists.

Go back a few paces then turn down Rue Keller. There you can visit (among others) **Galeries Est,**

July Column, Place de la Bastille

Job'Art, **Magda** and **Keller**. Go to the end and turn right on Rue de Charonne and up the atmospheric old passageway at No 37 to **Leif Ståhle**, a gallery run by the Swedish director of the Art Fair of Stockholm.

Back on Charonne, **Lavignes Bastille** is one of the best-known galleries in the neighbourhood. Andy Warhol has exhibited here. A few paces further, down the Passage Thiéré, is a tiny shop selling hand-crafted American objects called **Tumbleweed**, which might be just the thing if you are an American in Paris wanting to buy a gift. This is also the street for Latin American dance.

The last street on our agenda is Rue de Lappe, on the right off Charonne. There are more galleries here, including **Galerie la Bastille** and **Claire Burus**. Of course, exhibitions change regularly, so it is impossible to predict exactly what you will find. Prices may be negotiable.

Rue de Lappe is a good place to stop for dinner and have some fun, too. Try eating at **La Galoche**, right at the start of the street. The restaurant's name comes from the word for 'shoe' used in the region of Auvergne. It was outsiders from that province of France who first settled into the neighbourhood, and there are still signs of their influence in the speciality groceries and the faded signs hanging above the shops. La Galoche serves typical hearty fare from the region (150–200 Francs) in a warm friendly atmosphere. You can even purchase a pair of the wooden shoes here.

Such shoes, however, are not recommended for a night of dancing at the **Balajo**, three-quarters of the way down. This fun club is authentic and inexpensive, with its Art Deco look and big dance floor. It is one of the few night spots open on Monday, which is accordion night. Rumba, salsa, java and old rock and roll set

Rue de Lappe delicatessen

the beat. The crowd gets a bit rowdy at times, but the local renewal has tamed the ambience. In the Balajo, you know you are in Paris, for there is nothing anonymous about it.

If your day's journey has left you tired, you'll be glad to hear that you are almost back at the Place de la Bastille, and can head for the comfortable seats in the **Brasserie Bofinger** (5-7 Rue de la Bastille, just off to the west side of the Place), one of the city's finest. Settle back in the old-fashioned décor of brass, mirrors, leather and ceramics. The food is worthy of the oldest brasserie in town. For 200–250 Francs per person, you can enjoy a real feast; the menu features fresh seafood, *choucroute*, and traditional French dishes and wine.

Bois to Eiffel: Western Paris

Today's itinerary features a part of Paris known by its district number – the 16th – and largely ignored by tourists. It is a luxurious residential area bordering on the spacious western park of Paris, the Bois de Boulogne. Down by the riverside, the district puts on a much more familiar face at Trocadéro, where the monumental and museum-laden Palais de Chaillot opens its two wings to frame the city's most famous landmark: the Eiffel Tower. This is a long itinerary; you can lessen the walk by starting at the Musée Marmottan, missing the Bois altogether.

On a map, the **Bois de Boulogne** is a large green rectangle bordered on the far western side by a bend in the Seine River and on the inner side by the 16th district of Paris. The main road-entrance to the 2,000-acre (872 ha) park is at **Porte Dauphine** (Metro: Porte Dauphine). Start off early and walk along the Route de Suresne, or adventure off the roadway onto the footpaths leading to the **Lac Inférieur**, a long and narrow artificial lake.

In the Bois de Boulogne

You will share your morning stroll with many Parisians. There are always joggers out here, and the lake is popular with rowers. In some parts of the Bois, prostitution is practised rather openly by 'hitchhikers' standing near the roadway. By day, of course, this phenomenon is rarer.

You may see people waiting for the horses to start running at the **Auteuil Race Track**, studying their racing forms and the sports pages. Rose lovers should walk deeper into the park along the Route aux Lacs and the Route de Bagatelle to the **Bagatelle Gardens**. This fragrant park has long been a favourite spot for romance. The expression, *faire la bagatelle,* is a quaint way of saying 'make love'.

Children should head northward to the **Jardin d'Acclimatation** (Metro: Porte Maillot or Sablons). For a small entrance fee, you can visit the collection of farm animals and climb, roll, swing, slide, run, crawl and jump on a great collection of toys. For the price of tokens purchased inside, you can board the miniature train, visit a children's museum, and go on carousel rides. The garden has an old-fashioned atmosphere, reinforced by the people who frequent it: this is the haunt of wealthy white-gloved grandmothers from the 16th *arrondissement* with their tots dressed in navy blue sailor suits, girls in long braids and lace collars.

When you are ready to leave the Bois, amble down the footpath known as the Allée aux Dames which leads away from the Lac Inférieur. This heads over the traffic to the **Fortifications**, named after an archaeological site revealing the last remains of the old city wall. Walk out by the Route des Lacs where it leads to the Place de la Porte de Passy. Cut straight across the wide Boulevard Suchet and veer left on Avenue Ingres into the **Jardins de Ranelagh** (Metro: Ranelagh).

The trees seem to form a vaulting ceiling, green and airy, above the soft sandy floor, transforming the sedate little park into a cathedral. This is home to the **Musée Marmottan** (10am–5pm, closed Monday), discreetly sited on a corner on the north side of the park. The museum is devoted to the work of Impressionist painter Claude Monet. Delicious and colourful as summer itself, works from the last 20 years of his life make up the collection. Downstairs, in a specially designed room, are the painter's renowned *Water Lilies*, giant canvases done in his garden in Giverny. Also on display is the Marmottan family's collection of furniture and medieval manuscripts. Oddly enough, the different types of art seem quite at home together in this lovely old building.

Walk out of the triangular-shaped park by its tip on Chaussée de la Muette and straight ahead through one of the busiest intersections

of the 16th, **La Muette** (Metro: La Muette).

A telling story about this wealthy, rather snobbish part of town: when first incorporated into the city, the area was designated district number 13. Well-to-do residents didn't appreciate the unlucky number, and they used their collective political clout to have it changed. Still today, the very buildings evoke privilege, with their massive wooden doors, decorative carved facades – the

The Marmottan, for Monet

Statue of Balzac

architect's name is often engraved by the doorway – and manicured flower beds. *Au pair* girls guide small children across the street; maids go shopping with *Madame's* list in hand.

Around **Place de Passy** the shopping is made busier than ever by the covered market. Here elegant ladies look over the roast beefs and pinch avocados as they plan their dinner parties. Teenagers turned out in the latest fashions stop in chic little bakeries. Take the pedestrian street which leads off the little square (Passy), the Rue de l'Annonciation, which is often lined with interesting market stalls. Follow it down to the Rue Raynouard (Metro: Passy). At the end of the street, past Notre Dame de Grace de Passy, turn right. **Maison de Balzac** (10am–5.40pm, closed Monday) is on your left, lending a bit of high-spirited irreverence to the posh neighbourhood. The prolific writer lived here from 1840 to 1847, while revising the 90 volumes of his novel series *La Comédie Humaine*. Downstairs, the complex genealogy of the 2,000-odd characters has been mapped out, and Balzac's corrections appear in the margins of original manuscripts. One look at his cramped writing and the extensive annotations and

Balzac's home

you understand why typesetters charged double to do his books!

Balzac liked to work from 2am to 5pm. He kept going by drinking gallons of black coffee which he concocted himself, which explains the prominent coffee pot. Another feature of the house is the secret exit onto a back street. Without a secretary or an answering machine, he had his own way of escaping unwelcome callers.

Return on the Rue Raynouard through the appartment blocks to the tiny Passage des Eaux, on the right, which descends steeply to Charles Dickens Square. The **Musée du Vin** (noon–6pm, with its own restaurant at around 100 Francs per head) is located here. This simple little museum is very aptly situated, for the cellar cut into the riverbank hillside that once belonged to the monks of Passy, who made their own wine and stored it there 400 years ago. In the 17th century, the street was crowded with people coming to drink the mineral water flowing from the ground, reputed to have miraculous curative powers. It became a fashionable spot for lovers to meet, and Napoleon himself was seen here frequently.

During the French Revolution, the last monks were chased from the abbey and the convent was destroyed. None of the other buildings survived past 1906. The cellars were mostly forgotten until the 1960s when the owner of the Eiffel Tower Restaurant started storing his wine there. The present museum opened in 1984.

View from the Totem

The exhibits are a hodge-podge of tools, containers and wax figures; the walls are covered with engravings and drawings relating to wine. The boutique has a selection of vintage wines and all sorts of cork screws, serving baskets, glasses, decanters, thermometers, books, racks – everything to bring out the oenophile in you. And if it is all too much to resist, you can wind up with a little wine-tasting right on the spot.

It is a short walk (or one stop on the Metro from Passy) from the wine museum to **Place du Trocadéro** at the end of Boulevard Delessert. Follow the garden path up to the **Palais de Chaillot** on the hilltop. In the centre of the park, steps and ramps are alive with fountains and kids on roller-skates and skateboards.

The outdoor restaurant on the left is called the **Totem**, reached by taking the entrance to the Musée de l'Homme. The view over the gardens and across the river to the Eiffel Tower is enough to draw you in. The food is also worthwhile, a cut above the usual museum cafeteria. At about 150 Francs per person, it is one of the better deals in the neighbourhood.

Place du Trocadéro

The flat terrace between the two wings of Chaillot, lined with golden statuettes, is usually busy with African merchants selling bracelets, leather goods and toys. The curved buildings and monumental landscaping date from the World Fair of 1937. Now the complex is a formidable bastion of culture. It would be impossible to visit all of the exhibit space in one day, but each of these impressive museums deserves a mention (all are closed on Tuesday).

The **Musée de l'Homme** (10.30am–7pm) is devoted to anthropology. Eskimos, mummies, primitive man, mysterious civilisations, all have a place here. The **Salon de Musique** has a collection of musical instruments through the ages.

The **Musée des Monuments Français** in the north wing of the Palais is another favourite. Roman, Gothic and Renaissance architecture from all over France is represented. A place to wander in dreamily, it is like travelling through the French countryside of different eras.

A more recent arrival is the **Musée du Cinéma**. You must take a group tour with a guide, in accordance with the founder's wishes. If you love cinema and can understand some French, then you should line up for the one-hour trip through fantasy land. From flip cards and the first still photos, the history of cinema unfolds by way of landmarks like part of the set for Fritz Lang's *Metropolis*, Scarlet's green gown from *Gone With the Wind*, and a severed head from *Psycho*. Tours begin at 10 and 11am; then at 2, 3 and 4pm. The guides are thoroughly familiar with the subject and if the group is lively and talkative, the tour may go on longer than the planned hour.

Musée des Monuments details

Also on the hilltop is the **National Popular Theatre** (or Théâtre de Chaillot), which is so big it makes you feel as if you have walked into the belly of a whale. The main house seats 1,150; classical works are usually performed. The foyer and the smaller house

(Gémier) show less intimidating pieces. Finally, the **Musée de la Marine**, a maritime museum, makes a special effort for children.

Now, before your eyes as you cross the Seine looms the **Eiffel Tower**. The 1,050-ft (320-m) Tower, once vilified, now reigns as the queen of Parisian monuments. A recent face-lift in time for the Tower's 100th birthday coincided with the expiration of a privately held lease. The beauty treatment removed tons of rust and a sagging restaurant. New lights paint the metal lattice-work silver and gold at night.

Be prepared to stand in line during the summer or major holidays. The glass-walled elevator jerks up at an alarming angle. The machinery is unique in the world; a special team of employees does nothing but oversee spare parts, which must be made individually.

On the first level, an exhibit and short film recount the story of Gustave Eiffel and the 1889 World Fair. The Tower was meant to be temporary, and no one ever intended that it should become the symbol for Paris. In fact it was the advent of radio transmission and the need to site an aerial which gave the Tower, the world's highest structure when first built, a reason to stay.

The Eiffel Tower was once the material for an outrageous scam. A clever con man convinced victims that the Tower was to be torn down and, acting as a government agent, said he was authorised to arrange its sale as scrap iron. His first two victims were too embarrassed to expose him; the third was less proud!

Also on the first level is restaurant **La Belle France**; always full, so call ahead. Diners come more for the view than the food, which is not outstanding (at about 300 Francs per person).

On the top platform is another restaurant, much better than the first. You reach **The Jules Verne** by a private elevator for patrons only. Here too, reserve well in advance to savour the fine *cuisine traditionnelle*. Prices are among the highest in Paris.

The Tower is open until 11pm weekdays; till midnight on Friday, Saturday and before holidays. Tickets are a different price for each level. The long park stretching away from the riverside and under the Tower's splayed feet is the **Parc du Champs de Mars** (Metro: Bir-Hakeim or Ecole Militaire), once a military drill field. At the far end is the 18th-century **Ecole Militaire**, France's officer-training academy.

A final recommendation is to walk some distance down the colourful and varied **Rue St Dominique**, which is about half-way down the park on the left. At No 79, stop in at **Thoumieux,** another sort of Parisian landmark (Metro: Invalides). Open daily, their speciality is *cassoulet*, based on white beans and duck. The ambience is as appetising as the food. Informal and inexpensive, dinner costs about 150 Francs per person.

The symbol of Paris

Pick & Mix

Morning Itineraries

1. From Rodin to Dior

The 7th and 8th districts of Paris, separated by the Seine, are elegant neighbourhoods. This morning you will walk in beauty: start amongst the sublime forms in the Rodin Museum then move north via the Invalides to the river; stop by the Grand and Petit Palais, then on to Avenue Montaigne for haute couture.

The **Rodin Museum**, at 77 Rue de Varenne, opens at 10am (Metro: Varenne; closed on Tuesday). In the morning, the rose garden and its still pools are shadowed by the **Hôtel Biron**, built in 1731 as a private residence. August Rodin lived and worked there more than one hundred years later, and bequeathed it to the State on the condition that his works be exhibited in the house and park. Though he is now recognised as one of the greatest sculptors of all time, with a technique comparable to that of Michelangelo, Rodin was a figure of controversy in his own lifetime. Some of the early exhibitions of his work brought cries of fraud from 'experts' who

The Rodin Museum, in the Hôtel Biron

From Rodin to Dior

0.25 miles / 400 m

claimed that his human figures were so precise they could only have been made by using real bodies to form moulds for casting. In this setting, more than any other, the timeless figures do seem to live and breathe, calling out for caresses.

You enter under the gaze of what may be Rodin's most famous statue, *The Thinker*, set up high amid the greenery. To the left, *The Burghers of Calais* re-enact the noble gesture that saved their town from the ravages of the English army in the 14th century. Against the wall, *The Gates of Hell* is a monumental work wreathed with shapes of demons and the damned.

Inside the house, the wooden floors, marble staircase, gilt mirrors and French windows embrace large works, including the prominently displayed *Adam and Eve*, as well as small ones, such as *The Kiss*, a delicate study in white marble. There are works by other artists, including Camille Claudel, Rodin's assistant and mistress. The difficulties of the creative life were multiplied for her as a woman, and she eventually lost her mind and was all but forgotten in a mental institution. The film *Camille*, starring Isabelle Adjani and Gerard Depardieu, created renewed interest in the artist and her relationship with the great master.

Out the back door, you can wander under the grape arbour and rest on a sunny bench in this remarkable place, so full of peace and so fraught with turbulent feeling.

When you leave the *Hôtel*, turn left onto Boulevard des Invalides and walk to **Place Vauban**. Here you have a fine architectural vista offered by the Avenue de Breteuil, stretching out like a green carpet in one direction, and the giant complex known as **Les Invalides** on the other.

The first building that stands out is the golden-domed **Church of St Louis**, completely regilded as part of the city's bicentennial facelift in 1989. Therein lies the **Tomb of Napoleon I**, six layers of coffins beneath a

Church of St Louis

sarcophagus of dark red stone. He is kept company by a number of great generals and his son, the ill-fated 'King of Rome'. The decoration inside the church is distinctly military: flags captured from enemies of the Empire are hung on the walls.

The other vast wings of the Invalides were initially built as a veterans' home, but today's old soldiers make do with more commonplace housing, while the buildings house the **Army Museum** and administrative offices.

The museum is the world's largest of its kind, and exhibits cover everything from cannons and suits of armour to the taxi cabs mobilised for the Marne offensive in World War I. In the summer, a nightly sound and light show conjures up the glory days (check the announcements out front for times and languages).

Napoleonic images of grandeur are projected beyond the main entrance across the windswept **Esplanade des Invalides**. Both sides

Cannon detail

of the streets lead away to many government ministries, embassies and official residences. The *ensemble* culminates in the **Pont Alexandre III**, perhaps Paris's most splendid bridge (Metro: Invalides). Built in 1900, the bridge spans the Seine with a single metal arc. The golden statues and distinctive lamp-posts, backed by the domes of the Grand Palais, are pure Paris.

Crossing the river, you arrive right in the middle of the **Grand Palais** and the **Petit Palais**. Both are museums with permanent and changing exhibits (both closed on Tuesday). Look at the big posters outside to find out what's on. Occasional blockbuster shows bring crowds that form into a long line wrapped all the way around the park. These typical turn-of-the-century wrought-iron and glass 'crystal palaces' were built for the 1889 World Fair. The gardens around them are pleasant and shady; I suggest you take a breather and people-watch (Metro: Franklin D Roosevelt or Champs Elysées Clemenceau).

You'll need your breath for exclamations on the last leg of this

Bateau Mouche tour

itinerary: the main branch of 'The Golden Triangle' of shopping streets: **Avenue Montaigne**. Here you can gaze at the displays set up for Chanel, Cartier, Dior, Vuitton, Nina Ricci, Ungaro, Valentino... and more than your combined credit cards could imagine. Even if you don't venture into the boutiques, you can get an eyeful just strolling down the street, which is of course kept spotlessly clean and often decorated in holiday style by the high-tone tenants.

This brings you back to the riverbank at **Alma Marceau** (Metro: Pont d'Alma), where you can stop in a café or brasserie for lunch, or head for a **Bateau Mouche** tour boat just underneath the bridge. You can pick up a snack as you wait for the departure, and spend a pleasant hour off your feet, gliding by the scenery. Boats leave every 20 minutes or so in summer; nighttime batteries of lights illuminate the riverside architecture. Don't bother trying to listen to the static and crackle of the multi-lingual, taped commentary, just sit back and look. Sure, it's touristy, but even nonchalant Parisians enjoy the unique view from the water.

Pont Alexandre III, the most splendid bridge in Paris

2. Père Lachaise

This suggestion for a peaceful morning in eastern Paris takes you to a resting place for the famous and a Parisian village.

Those who know it love to return, and some who go there never leave – such as Frédéric Chopin, Molière, Rossini, and more recent luminaries including Edith Piaf, Gertrude Stein, Oscar Wilde and Jim Morrison. The place, of course, is the **Père Lachaise Cemetery**, in eastern Paris, the city's largest and loveliest burial ground (Metro: Père Lachaise).

At the main entrance on Boulevard de Menilmontant, visitors can pick up a map with the locations of the more famous graves, and the small bookstore also sells a surprising variety of guides to the cemetery. Indeed, most of the people wandering about seem more curious than bereaved.

At first glance, this older part of the cemetery near the entrance appears to make use of above-ground burial, but look closely and you'll see that the tiny houses in this city of the dead are actually small chapels, often in disrepair. Walk up Avenue Principale and turn right to find the monument marking the grave of Héloïse and Abelard. She was a student of the controversial theologian in the 12th century, and secretly became his wife. Her father's fury separated them, he (castrated) in a monastery and she in a convent, but they left their letters to posterity, professing a pure and faithful love.

Chopin's tomb

Make your way along the shady paths to the chapel on the hilltop for a view over the stalwart chestnut trees, spreading like guardian spirits over the myriad monuments. You may see the benches occupied by old women feeding the many cats who make their homes amongst the monuments.

Others come to visit the grave of Allan Kardec, spiritualist, and leave odd mementos or practice bizarre rites in front of his tomb.

Of historic interest is the **Mur des Fédérés**, at the back of the cemetery in its eastern corner where grotesque and striking war memorials spring from the earth.

The wall was where the last of the anarchist rebels of the *Commune de Paris,* a courageous uprising against Prussian domination in 1871, were lined up and shot. The bullet holes are still visible. Also in this top corner is the Jardin du Souvenir, with many monuments to the dead of World War II. Some of the works in memory of those who died in Nazi concentration camps are frightening reminders of that horror, dedicated to the victims of Auschwitz, Ravensbruck, Buchenwald and others. There are also monuments to different members of the French Resistance. If you are especially interested in this period, you may be able to meet war veterans or historians here.

Leave the quiet behind slowly, exiting at this corner down the steps onto **Rue de la Réunion** (named after the Indian Ocean island which is a French territory), a street more full of baby strollers than cars. This is the sort of neighbourhood where people close up the shop and go home for lunch and a snooze, with a *baguette* of bread under the arm.

Keep going across Rue Bagnolet to **Place de la Réunion**, which looks as if it had been picked up and transported from some much smaller town in France, or even directly from the tropics, as the local African community adds a colourful dimension to the tiny circle and park. It may be ramshackle and not particularly elegant, but this is as much true Paris as the downtown boulevards.

Continue through this neighbourhood of small shops and furniture craftsmen down the Rue des Orteaux and just under the old train line into Rue du Clos. This takes you to **Le Village St Blaise**, tucked discreetly into this eastern end of Paris (Metro: Porte de Montreuil). Part of the neighbourhood is a modern public housing development and shopping centre with a purple colour scheme. The quality and originality of the architecture and planning belie the 'moderate rent' nature of the housing.

Turn left and walk up Rue St Blaise. Up here is a good find for lunch, an Algerian restaurant called **Le Village de Paris** (24 Rue St Blaise). *Couscous*, the main item on the menu, is very popular in Paris, and not only with the large North African population. This family restaurant is warm and homey. Big dishes are brought out to the table and you can garnish your plate as you choose with a selection of exotic appetizers. Then follows the *couscous:* four varieties of fluffy semolina, a bowl of piping hot vegetables and sauce; a little tub of hot pepper sauce for spice; and a choice of mutton, chicken or beef.

After the meal, pass around the plate of fresh dates. If you like Algerian food, head directly here, you can't find better, and you can't beat the prices (150 Francs gets you any dish on the menu).

There are other nice places on the street that you'll be tempted to discover yourself, and even a dainty tea room for delicate eaters further down (**Le Damier**).

Watching over Rue St Blaise, its single rose window like a benevolent eye, is **St Germain de Charonne**, whose country-church character suits the neighbourhood well. This church is so popular for weddings that Parisians sign up a year in advance for the pleasure of saying *oui* at the altar and having their wedding pictures taken out front.

Walk up the steps on its left side, and take a look at the cemetery – quite a contrast to Père Lachaise. From here the Rue des Prairies and Rue des Pyrénées will take you back to **Place Gambetta**, the heart of the 20th *arrondissement*, and the Metro.

3. Shopping Tour

Looking for a special gift? Feeling guilty about leaving the kids behind? Ready to brave the fashion boutiques? Follow this trail. If you're a window shopper only, this can easily be done in a morning, but if you go on a spree, it may take all day!

There's one Metro station in Paris that everyone seems to pass through regularly, and it bears the name of the famous building above it, the **Opéra**. It's a lively neighbourhood, the hub of the Grands Boulevards, and business centre to banks, travel companies, and the nearby Stock Exchange (La Bourse).

If you need to replenish your wallet, stop off first at **American Express**, on Rue Scribe, with many services for travellers including banking and foreign exchange. Or if you're in a hurry and have cash, try the automatic money exchange machine at the BNP **Bank** right on the Place de l'Opéra. Twenty-

Buy a bit of elegance

four hours a day, you can slip your own currency in the slot and get Francs in return, or use your credit card. A wide variety of travel and ticket agents for tours and shows are here and in the surrounding streets.

Start your tour proper at the **Palais Garnier** (open 10am–6.30pm) as the Opéra building is officially known. This 'wedding cake' was completed in 1875, the crowning achievement of the plan designed by Haussmann to open up the centre of Paris.

You can walk into the vaulting foyer for a glimpse of the eclectic décor, and on days when no rehearsal is in progress, you can go into the theatre itself. A splendid surprise awaits you overhead: painter **Marc Chagall's ceiling**, a frolicsome work in blue and pearl tones, in striking contrast to the sombre red and gold opulence of the hall.

Just across the street is the **Grand Hotel**, and its sidewalk café, the **Café de la Paix**, one of the most celebrated in Paris. This is a prime spot for indulging in the art of seeing and being seen, or completing a *rendezvous*.

The expansive (and expensive!) café, taking up a whole corner of the Place de l'Opéra, is not the place to go when you're in a hurry, but, as its name suggests, a venue for a moment of peace in the midst of the crowd. If you really need to get out of the fray, there's a cosy bar tucked away on the far side of the main hall of the hotel. The bartenders there have invented a few special cocktails that you won't forget.

Revived and refreshed, head for *Les Grands Magasins*. These department stores sprang up in Paris in the last century and have been popular ever since. On Boulevard Haussmann you'll find the **Galeries Lafayette** first of all. Walk in and orient yourself by heading for the central escalators and the store directory in French and English, plus a bilingual hostess who can help you find that perfect gift. Other services at the store include a fashion consultant, currency exchange, and duty free forms for recovering sales taxes at the airport. Fashion is the biggest seller here, whether it's off-the-rack designer or the Galeries' own label. Accessories are fun shopping: stockings,

Printemps

scarves, headwear and other items you never knew you needed before.

Across the street is **Marks and Spencers**, the British chain store, which seems just as popular as its French cousins. And another block down is **Printemps**, which has advertised itself as 'the most Parisian department store'. It certainly is the most beautiful inside: the domed ceiling built in 1923 is now classified as a historic monument. The perfume department has the largest selection in Paris. There are make-up demonstrations and fashion shows scheduled almost every day, and you find the same services for English-speaking tourists as in the Galeries.

The street along the two stores takes up the overflow of commerce and all along the pavements you'll be entertained by fast and furious sales pitches for such essentials as revolutionary cookware, two-for-one deals of a lifetime, and the latest development in travel irons. There are plenty of odd-lots and bargains for those who can withstand the pressure of the crowd flowing by.

Jump out of the main stream of traffic onto the pedestrian **Rue de Caumartin** (Metro: Havre-Caumartin). There is more room to breathe on this street, bordered by smaller shops and the 18th-century **St Louis d'Antin church**. Free organ concerts are regularly scheduled on weekends; leaflets inside the main entrance give the dates. More spontaneous street music concerts are likely to be in progress at any time.

Just beyond the church, look carefully for the entrance to the **Passage du Havre**, on the left. This covered gallery is undergoing redevelopment. It leads to the **Gare St Lazare** train station (Metro:

Galeries Lafayette, where fashion is the biggest seller

St Lazare). Turn right on Rue d'Amsterdam and walk up some distance past Place de Budapest until you see the sign for **Androuët** on the left (No 41).

This small shop is known for selling the finest cheeses in Paris. There is a wonderful old-fashioned restaurant upstairs with a menu devoted to dishes with cheese in the recipe. At the last count, there were about 300 varieties offered. Why not go for the *dégustation unique de tours de fromage*, loosely translated as 'all the cheese you can eat!' Of course, there is a good wine list to complement the savoury fare. The set menu is moderately-priced, and luncheon *à la carte* costs between 150-300 Francs per person.

But if you're not ready to interrupt your shopping, or if you still haven't found what you're looking for, continue your shopping tour back down Rue Tronchet and Rue Vignon, which lead from St Lazare to the Place de la Madeleine. **Rue Vignon** in particular has smaller boutiques without the designer names of the Avenue Montaigne, but with interesting ideas and prices. For unusual little gifts to take home, I recommend **La Maison du Miel** (24 Rue Vignon), offering a variety of French honey in pretty little pots, and other products such as soaps and shampoos.

The Ritz Hotel

The monumental church in the centre of **Place de la Madeleine** (Metro: La Madeleine) is not very welcoming. You'd be better employed giving your attention to the window displays at **Fauchon**, which will leave no doubt in your mind in regard to French supremacy in the art of presenting food. You can have lunch here *sur le pouce* (informally), a favourite with people who work in the neighbourhood: just point at what looks good to you behind the glass cases, an employee will pile it up on a plate for you and you can eat (standing up) at the counter.

If you would rather picnic, head for the nearby Tuileries after a stop at one of the other exotic food shops on the Place de la Madeleine, (try **Hediard**, where they wrap your purchases in chic black and red paper and ribbon) to fill your basket with caviar, tropical fruits, and a vintage wine.

The **Rue Faubourg St Honoré** and **Rue St Honoré** continue the chic shopping. These streets are the traditional (if somewhat outmoded) address for major designers like **Hermès** and **Gucci**. Just around the corner is the **Place Vendôme**, elegantly symmetrical and home to the Ritz Hotel and **Cartier** jewellers, whose major outlet is nearby on Rue de la Paix.

If you've still got money left then end your day with tea at the **Ritz** (proper attire required) or something stronger in the hotel's **Hemingway Bar**, named after the writer who made it his hangout.

Afternoon Itineraries

4. Montmartre and Pigalle

Montmartre, perched on a steep hill on the northern rim of Paris, is a legend in itself. It seems to have its own history apart from the city below, its own famous citizens, and its own traditions in entertainment and art. The Sacré Coeur Basilica, a landmark which can be observed from all over the city, is the central tourist site, but not really the heart of its neighbourhood. Be warned: free maps don't show the narrow streets of this itinerary.

Montmartre is known for its artists

I should just say that Montmartre is almost always very crowded with tourists. But, surprisingly, a walk of a few blocks away from the central Place du Tertre brings you to quiet streets where stairs tumble down to the city below, quiet as the cats prowling about. If stairs and steep hills are too much for you, I'd recommend the Montmartrobus, a special bus line that runs between Pigalle and the hilltop. For the cost of one Metro ticket for a one-way trip, it is the best tour deal in town. Much the same route is also covered by a miniature train (Le Petit Train de Montmartre); the latter is cute, but no great improvement and more expensive.

Start the itinerary at the **Place d'Anvers** (Metro: Anvers). Follow the signs to the *Funiculaire* that lead you up the Rue Steinkerque. The street is lined with fabric and clothes shops. If you have an eye for that sort of thing, there are nice bits of velvet ribbon, fancy buttons and trims, something to take home. You can also find lacy curtains, so typical of Paris, with unusual motifs and designs.

At the top of the street, with Montmartre's white basilica rising above you, turn right to walk down to the **Marché**

St Pierre. This 19th-century covered marketplace has recently changed its vocation. It is now home to the **Primitive Art Museum** (*Musée d'Art Naïf – Max Fourny*), which presents works by artists from around the world, painting in the colourful, magical style that Rousseau made famous. The small new museum also offers children's workshops, and the bookshop has an original selection of books, cards and ideas for manual activities for children. Look out for postcards which the recipient can cut out into earrings.

Above the green park bordering the Place St Pierre looms the **Sacré Coeur** ('sacred heart') **Basilica**, which was built a mere century ago – small potatoes in this city. Its construction came on the heels of the *Commune de Paris* uprising against Prussian domination in 1871. The uprising took its inspiration and strength from Montmartre and its anarchist population, who resisted to the last. It was French regular troops who betrayed the *Communards*, executing 25,000 of them in the final weeks of battle.

The church was built in appeasement for the bloodshed, and so has never been well-loved by local residents, known as *Montmartrois*. To this day, it is often mocked in cabaret songs on the hilltop (locally known as *La Butte*).

Climb the switchback stairway, or relax in the **Funicular railway** (use one Metro ticket) to reach the terrace in front of Sacré Coeur. From here you have a splendid view over the city, and coin-operated telescopes to help you pick out your favourite places. Look

Sacré Coeur Basilica, a Parisian landmark

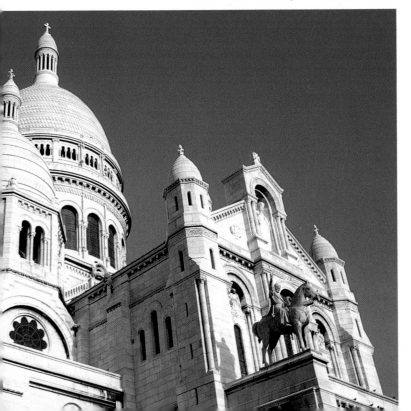

straight out directly south into the centre of Paris, and you should easily distinguish the brightly-coloured Pompidou Centre and the two square towers of Notre Dame, which stand out from the otherwise remarkably low-rise and uniform city centre. This vista is just at the opposite side of Paris from the panorama seen at the top of the Montparnasse Tower (*Day 1*). The Tower is off to the right, black and solitary on the skyline.

Now walk around to the right behind the church. It is like going behind a curtain and discovering a magical theatre set. Follow the lane round to the left and the **Place du Tertre** greets you with strings of bright lights and swirls of colourful people. You'll return to the square later. Battling through the crowds towards the *point de vue* on the corner of Rue Poulbot you will find the new Espace Montmartre, home of over 300 works by **Salvador Dalí**, and its popular shop. The museum is open daily between 10am and 6pm.

Stroll down Rue du Mont Cenis; leaving the crowd behind, and take a left on Rue Cortot. No 6 was the house Eric Satie lived in while composing his delightful piano pieces. The painter Utrillo, who captured so many of *La Butte's* houses and cafés in his work, also lived on this street, with his mother, artist Suzanne Valdon.

At No 12 is the **Musée de Montmartre** (11am–5.30pm, closed Monday) settled in an 18th-century manor house along with the **Montmartre Cultural Centre**. Its windows look over the **Montmartre Vineyards** and Rue St Vincent. Every October, there is a big harvest celebration here.

Obviously, given the size of the vineyard, there is not a lot of wine bottled, and its value is more sentimental than gustatory. But

Place du Tertre, Montmartre

it is a great source of pride to the *Montmartrois*, proving that the folks who live up here still have a strong community spirit. On the lower floors of the museum, you can see re-creations of the study of composer and violinist Gustave Charpentier, and a typical cabaret. The graceful garden setting and the care with which original objects have been preserved and presented make this the best museum to visit in Montmartre. It sums up the long history and special character of the 'village' well.

Go to the end of Rue Cortot and turn right onto Rue des Saules. The vineyards are visible from down here for those who didn't go into the museum, with the Montmartre Cemetery behind its wall diagonally across from the vines. A bit further down is **Le Lapin Agile** (22 Rue des Saules, Metro: Lamarck-Caulaincourt), an old-fashioned cabaret which opens at 9pm, and the last show ends at 2am. The entrance price gets you a spot on a long wooden bench by a scarred table, and a little glass of cherries in *eau-de-vie*. All night long, guests are treated to 'songs, humour and poetry', in the tradition established here by Aristide Bruant, who was immortalised by the Toulouse-Lautrec portrait showing him in his perpetual black hat and cape. Many of the roving performers sing songs he composed as they make the rounds of cabarets on the *Butte*. Le Lapin sounds quaint, but it is also fast-paced, and you'd have to have good knowledge of French to appreciate it.

Back up the hill, the restaurant **La Maison Rose** on the corner was the subject of the painting that brought fame to Utrillo. Left at the Maison Rose leads to an elegant corner called the **Allée des Brouillards**. Ivy-covered gates stand before snug houses and their neat gardens. The **Château des Brouillards** (Castle of the Mists) stands opposite, in a small

Le Lapin Agile, old-fashioned cabaret

park. The house was built in 1772 by an actor from the Comédie Française, and several artists lived in it during the years that followed. Now boarded up, it is a spooky place, haunted by the souls of poets.

Go down the steps of Rue Girardon to Avenue Junot. Stop in the **aa galerie**, a friendly shop that has taken as its mission the revival of the artistic tradition of Montmartre. Besides showing art, they also run music and poetry nights, and dabble in theatre and debate.

Follow the curving Avenue Junot back up to Girardon and Rue Lepic; at the crossroads stands the **Moulin de la Galette**. The windmill was made into a dance hall in the 19th century, and celebrated in a painting by Renoir. Vincent Van Gogh lived with his brother in a pretty little house at No 54 Rue Lepic.

Go across Lepic into a little alley called Rue d'Orchampt, and follow it round. At the end there is a row of artists' studios that look much like the old **Bateau Lavoir** did when Picasso and Braque painted there. The site of their Montmartre studios is around the corner on **Place Emile Goudeau** (Metro: Abbesses).

Of course, many of the famous artists who lived and loved in Montmartre – Picasso, Apollinaire, Matisse, Toulouse-Lautrec, Marie Laurencin, to name only a few – were also great *bons vivants*. A good time is still on the agenda, and to make the most of your night out, I have three suggestions to suit your style.

Back in Place du Tertre I recommend **A La Mère Catherine** (on the square). This is the classic French restaurant. The décor is dignified and warm, the menu is simple and inviting. The years haven't changed much about this place at all; it's not unusual to see three generations sitting at the same table, and no one looks out of place. (About 150 Francs per person).

Another more informal option is **Tartempion**, on Rue du Mont Cenis, serving plain fare and tasty desserts at moderate prices (100 – 150 Francs). On a warm night you can sit outdoors on the terrace with a view of the street as it abruptly ends in a stairway, and the city lights floating in space beyond.

After dinner, I suggest you stay on the *Butte* and head for **La Bohème du Tertre**. You can't miss this brightly lit cabaret on a corner of Place du Tertre. Head for the back room where musicians play traditional dance music (polka, waltz, and a Charleston or two). The crowd really gets going with French drinking songs and old songs about Montmartre. Order a bottle of wine and dance and sing until 2am.

Alternatively, there are famous and racier venues nearby. Come down off the hilltop and out of the shadow of the church to head for the naughtier regions of lower Montmartre and Pigalle. Take the twisty Rue Lepic all the way to Place Blanche (Metro: Blanche),

Transport to La Bohème du Tertre

where you will find the unmistakable **Moulin Rouge**. Skip the dinner show here, the food is dull and the prices high, but take a look at the photos for fun, and buy a ticket for later if you're interested. The Moulin has been showing feathers and skin for 100 years now, so must be doing something right. Continue on down the sexy Boulevard de Clichy to the **Place de Clichy** (Metro: Place de Clichy) and the restaurant **Charlot Roi des Coquillages**. The speciality is seafood, enticingly displayed on ice. Raw oysters are said to stimulate the libido, just right for a night in this neighbourhood! The *bouillabaisse* (an intricate and hearty fish soup) has a good reputation. Count on up to 250 Francs for a meal with wine; you have until 1am to finish it.

Also on Place de Clichy is **Wepler**, the oyster bar and restaurant favoured by author Henry Miller when he sowed his wild oats in this part of town. Open until 1.30am, Wepler is similar in price to Charlot (set menu 150 Francs).

After dinner, you can backtrack to Blanche and continue all the way to **Pigalle** (Metro: Pigalle), known to WWII soldiers as 'Pig Alley'. Along the way, there are plenty of strip shows and hawkers to lure you inside. The entrance fee to these places is next to nothing, but the drinks served inside are obligatory and expensive.

Pigalle is changing all the time; **Folies Pigalle**, for example, has gone from sex show to alternative theatre to music hall. Rock clubs offer a different brand of entertainment and attract a new crowd. **La Locomotive** (90 Blvd de Clichy) goes full steam ahead until 5.30am. It is a lot bigger than the Folies, has two separate discos, two bars, a video room and live music. And when the club closes, you can go back up the hill for sunrise!

One hundred years of feathers, skin and sin

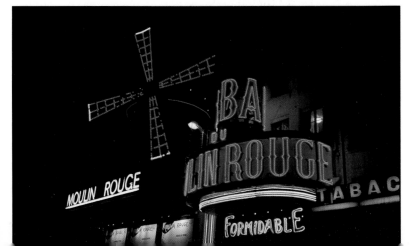

5. By Canal to La Villette

The canals of Paris? Yes indeed, and although there are no singing gondoliers, there are locks and barges, and a very particular urban landscape. What used to be a trade lifeline has now been restored for leisure use. Discover this surprising waterway, and the modern new museum complex that has been built along its banks, Parc de la Villette. This is a good itinerary for children, particularly if you are tired of walking.

Redevelopment of the area around La Bastille began with the improvement of the **Arsenal Marina** (Metro: Bastille). The Marina was once a very active commercial shipping port; adjacent to the Seine it joins the **Canal St Martin** leading eastward out of the city. At Bastille, the canal goes underground, emerging again beyond Place de la République. Board the **Canauxrama Tour Boat** (tel: 42391500) at Arsenal Marina, on the level of No 50 Blvd de la Bastille, for a three-hour journey eastward. Departures are at 9.30am and 2.30pm daily and the commentary is only in French.

Napoleon built the canal partly to get more water into the city centre and thus earn the citizen's affection; in those days average daily consumption was 1 litre (just over 2 pints) per person, as opposed to 200 litres today. As you glide under the city, the canal is lit by sidewalk gratings sending eerie shafts of light down to the water. The different colours of mortar indicate where restoration work has been done; directly overhead has been untouched since the canal was built. Classical music from the boat echoes through the tunnel.

Arsenal Marina

The Géode – circular projection screen

At Quai Valmy and Quai de Jemmapes, you emerge in trees and gardens and yet another unique Parisian landscape. Wait patiently at the locks; note how the moss on the canal walls often hides fresh water mussels.

On the left bank, your guide will point out the **Hôtel du Nord**, and play part of the soundtrack. This was the setting for a French movie of the same name. When the hotel was recently slated for demolition, neighbours and cinephiles protested so strongly that the famous facade was saved.

Near the **Bassin de la Villette**, warehouses and cafés cater to the mainly leisure boating on the canal. Some of the industrial space here has been reclaimed by artists' cooperatives as studio space and undoubtedly this neighbourhood is in for some big changes in the years ahead. Just beyond the port, the canal divides into the Canal St Denis and the Canal de l'Ourcq, two working waterways.

This is the end of your boat ride. What you see all around you now is known as the **Parc de la Villette** (Metro: Porte de Pantin). It is a big cultural complex created in 1986 on the site of the city's former cattle market. The market building itself, a fine example of 19th century iron architecture to the right of the canal, is now an exhibition space, **La Grande Halle**. Exhibits here range from the prestigious and often controversial Paris Biennale contemporary art show to the International Architectural Fair, and even presentations of high fashion collections. There is a small space called **La Maison de la Villette** with a permanent exhibit on the history of La Villette and the market.

Walkway at La Villette

On the left of the canal, the **Géode**, a polished steel sphere that plays weird music, looks like something from outer space that just landed in a pond. Inside, the hemispheric theatre has one of the world's largest projection screens and dizzily slanted seating. Movies are made specially for these huge screens. Outside, photographers try to capture its mystery on film.

Reflected in the shiny steel is the **City of Science and Industry**. It takes hours to see the whole thing, and the entrance fee (45 Francs) is relatively high. The museum is usually open 10am–6pm Tuesday to Sunday. Even if you don't visit the whole thing, you can walk in the main hall for free and look at the exhibits on the ground floor. Brochures and cassette guides in English are available.

La Villette is devoted to science. One of the best parts is a big room for children (of all ages) where visitors participate in experiments using soap bubbles, mirrors, electricity, magnets and tricks of perspective. There is a jet pack simulator for armchair astronauts to simulate space travel.

Other exhibits cover the universe, the origins of life, the underwater world, plant life, and there are even animal robots in a cybernetic zoo. At every turn computer terminals inform and amuse.

Short films are shown in different areas, and the ultra-modern **Planetarium** runs several programmes a day (there is an extra charge. Get your tickets as soon as you arrive – they go fast).

In the park next to the northern bridge is a big, grey, square and solid-looking tent. This is the **Zenith Concert Hall**, which can seat up to 6,300 people. It has excellent acoustics and modern facilities, and is often booked for rock music.

La Villette is not the place for haute cuisine, but there's a selection of cafés and burger bars dotted through the park and in the city of sciences.

To get back into town from here, you can take the Metro from Porte de la Villette. Alternatively, a pleasant route is to take bus No 75, which goes right back to the Pompidou Centre and Hôtel de Ville. Pick it up at the **Place de la Porte de Pantin**, which you reach by turning left at the road entrance to the Grande Halle and walking up to the big roundabout. Like most of the Parisian buses, it runs until about 8.30pm; after that, you'll have to look for a taxi or use the Metro.

Passing time in the park

The bus route takes you past the hilly park of the **Buttes Chaumont**, built in an old quarry and planted in the English romantic style with trees, islands, and a little Greek temple just peeping through the trees atop its knoll.

Next the bus passes **Place du Colonel Fabian**, and the headquarters of the French Communist Party, designed by Brazilian architect Oscar Niemeyer. It goes back down to Place de la République and from there turns into the Marais district past the Pompidou Centre and on to the Hôtel de Ville. A short trip down busy Rue de Rivoli and the bus driver takes a break at the **Pont Neuf Bridge**; the name means 'New Bridge', but in fact it is the oldest in town, and one of the most remarkable. From the riverside, note the hundreds of faces carved along the side, each one unique.

6. The New Louvre

You may be startled to see references to the 'New Louvre' or Le Grand Louvre. What happened to the old Louvre? The answer is: a lot! Astonishing changes have been made, not without controversy but certainly with great success. The world's largest museum is still labyrinthine, but a joy to discover for old hands as well as first-time visitors. And only the French would be so bold as to completely redo their major world museum.

Le Grand Louvre is the name President François Mitterrand chose to designate his vast project of restructuring the huge palace and the museum inside. The first, much-delayed step involved prying the Finance Ministry out of its privileged digs in one wing. The second major step called on Chinese-American architect IM Pei to create a new entrance and orientation centre.

His design is already world-famous, and will certainly become part of the architectural legend of Paris. The large glass **Pyramid** rises in the middle of the **Cour Napoléon**. Around it are three smaller pyramids. The area between them is accented by flat, triangular basins in dark stone, raised

In the Louvre

slightly above the level of the ground. Fountains in these pools complete the composition.

The 'landscape', as Pei calls it, in the tradition of landscape artist Le Nôtre, was designed to bring light into the museum entrance below, and it also succeeds in lightening the whole courtyard and the stone façades surrounding it.

The thoughtful use of materials and colours allows the sky and

Inside the Louvre pyramid

water to become elements in the illusionistic space. The glass was specially developed and polished twice in France and England. It is held in place by stainless steel nodes and cables. The result is light and sparkling, a balance of reflection and transparency weighed against the thick stone facade of the old palace, which is heavy with centuries of history. This is the **main entrance** to the museum, but you may be able to dodge any queues by using the Richelieu Passage, off Rue de Rivoli and the Place du Palais Royal. The Louvre is open 9am–5.45pm, Thursday to Sunday; 9am–9.45pm on Monday and Wednesday, and is closed on Tuesday.

Go through the revolving door and turn down the spiral staircase. The central pillar is an ingenious elevator. This is the **Hall Napoléon** reception area. The din of milling visitors sounds like a swimming pool, but manages not to be overbearing and there is plenty of space.

The new museum services located here are excellent. Ticket windows, the information desk, a bookshop, the rest rooms, and the cafeteria are all easy to find and reach – already a big improvement over the 'old' Louvre! A sit-down restaurant and a sandwich bar provide other alternatives for hungry and thirsty visitors. A wall of screens lists the day's exhibits and activities, and rooms which may be temporarily closed. You will also find a post office, money changing facilities, a cloak room and even an infirmary on this level. The bookshop contains not only post cards and prints, but 15,000 books and periodicals in many languages. Casts of art works, jewellery and other gift items are also on sale.

English cassette tours are available, and there is a six-minute film presentation of some of the major works which can be viewed in the reception area. You can also take a tour with a guide.

When construction began on the new Louvre, major archaeological research was carried out. The fruit of these efforts is now on display in an underground exhibition area called the **Medieval Louvre**. Drawings and scale models show the Louvre at different stages of its career, and reveal how many transformations it had known prior to today. Walk around the ancient walls and most of the medieval fortress, past the towers that were once the gates to the city. The architectural prowess used to display the old foundations so effectively is breathtaking.

Elegant and light

There is an exhibition of some of the artifacts uncovered, including many ceramic pieces. The most splendid find was certainly the **Helmet of Charles VI**, found in barely recognisable bits and art-

The Louvre's most famous portrait

fully reproduced. It is on display in the **Salle Saint Louis**, perhaps the most impressive part of the newly opened area.

The Louvre, with these new openings and additions, is now bigger than ever, and it is impossible not to get lost. No matter which way you turn, you always seem to end up in the Egyptian Antiquities! However, like Alice in Wonderland, visitors need only wander at random to discover many marvels. The presence of the Pyramid, visible from many different angles from the tall windows, is of some help in orientation. On the ground floor, the **Oriental, Egyptian, Greek** and **Roman Antiquities** were the first items to be displayed. Many were brought back from Napoleon's campaigns.

The Egyptian section has, of course, mummies and cult objects, busts and statues of ancient rulers. This famous collection enables scholars to trace the whole development of Egyptian civilisation from prehistory to the Christian era.

Two very famous ladies grace the Greek and Roman rooms: *Venus de Milo* and *Winged Victory*. Their celebrity has somewhat overshadowed the rest. Vast, sunny and quiet, the proportions of the rooms are well suited to the pieces.

Although the outstanding part of this section is made up of sculpture, there are also bronzes, decorative and useful objects, tools, jewellery and bas-reliefs. Many are details taken from the city's various eras.

The second major section of the Louvre collection is **paintings**. These are from all the European schools, from the 13th to the 17th centuries, and they are displayed on the upper floors. Two-thirds are French, and include works by 17th- and 18th-century artists such as de la Tour, Poussin, Watteau and Fragonard; all to be visited in the **Grande Galérie**. This section's most famous resident is, of course, the *Mona Lisa*, in the company of an impressive gathering of other works by Leonardo da Vinci. Masterpieces by Raphael, Titian, and Veronese compete for the visitor's eye in these rooms.

Other crowd-stoppers are the large paintings in the **Pavillon Denon**, including *Napoleon Crowning Josephine* (David), *The Great*

Odalisque (Ingres), *The Raft of the Medusa* (Géricault), and the famous revolutionary and inspiring painting of *Liberty Leading the People* (Delacroix).

The third section is known as **Objets d'Art**, and includes furniture, jewellery and small statuary, much of it confiscated from royalty at the time of the Revolution. **Apollo's Gallery** is a beautiful room with an intricate ceiling painted by Delacroix. Glass cases display the remaining pieces of the Crown Jewels of France. The reputed Crown of St Louis sits besides Napoleon's coronation headgear. Numerous gem-encrusted and golden objects glitter beneath the guard's watchful eye. Less overwhelming, but just as admirable, is the collection of tapestries, furniture and clocks.

The great redistribution of paintings in the Louvre, now that more space is available, will take several years to complete. Eventually, paintings will be rearranged in a more chronological perspective, and according to national schools. Already works which were previously not hung for lack of space are on public view. In the new top-floor rooms, these include *The History of Alexander* by Le Brun, a series of huge paintings that have been rolled up for almost 30 years. Other works will be shown on a rotating basis as the program of redistribution is carried out. So even Louvre veterans should be prepared for some surprises.

7. La Défense

An afternoon at the avant-garde business district on the west side of the city centre. La Défense epitomises French commitment to grand and futuristic projects.

Take the RER line A to La Défense, the same line which – on the other side of Paris – travels out to Euro Disney. The two venues have something in common, because in both you emerge into completely new worlds, worlds which are hard to believe in when you come straight from downtown Paris.

At La Défense the station exits emerge into the **Les Quatre Temps** commercial centre, with shops and restaurants in a rather un-Parisian shopping-mall style. Head for the daylight, following signs to the **Grande Arche**. This latter building is at the top of the long flight of courtyards up the centre of the district, and is very simplistic in its architecture. If you climb the steps into the open centre (from where there are lifts to the top, 9am – 7pm Monday to Friday and until 8pm on Saturday and Sunday) stop after the last step to witness one of the most magnificent – and oldest – pieces of city planning in the world stretching below you. The

Grande Arche is at the end of an axis that runs straight as a dye down to the Arch de Triomphe, on down the Champs-Elysées, through Concorde and ends at the Arc de Triomphe du Carrousel, just in front of the Louvre. And this axis hasn't stopped growing yet: there are plans afoot to extend it further out to the west.

Acute observers will notice that the Grande Arche is in fact slightly at an angle to the axis (most visible from a ground plan). This could have been creative spin put on the building by Danish architect Johan Otto von Spreckelsen – but is in fact thanks to problems in siting the foundations. Even on the calmest of days the Grande Arche whispers with sea-noises, and the sense of peace that it emanates seems to bewitch even the pigeons.

Most of the buildings of La Défense are headquarters, and are often clearly labelled as so. Fourteen out of the top 20 French companies have their main offices here, as do 13 out of the top 50 companies in the world. And even though the *Grand Projet* of La Défense was officially completed in 1988 after 20 years, many of the original buildings are now being replaced with bigger, better and more advanced constructions. In all, some 100,000 people work at La Défense for around 1,300 companies, and the area is also home to some 35,000 residents who live mainly on the outer sides or behind, in the landscaped park district.

On a fine day La Défense is a very pleasant place to be. Wander down from the Grande Arche looking at the sculptures (there are over 70 signed pieces on the premises – including what looks like a group of large nasal hairs in tubes). Half-way down, the fountains are orchestrated into water-ballets at certain times of the day.

On a wet day the weather can turn the open area into a deserted canyon of architecture; you could do worse than scurry into the **Dôme IMAX**, a hemispherical cinema. There is also a programme of arts for which you will need to consult the local press.

The Grande Arche at La Défense

EXCURSIONS

The region immediately surrounding the city of Paris is called the *Ile de France*, and is rich in history and culture. Some of the most popular spots are also the most accessible, and typical French countryside is never far away. The following destinations can easily visited in a day. If you leave Paris before noon, you can be back in time for dinner.

8. Versailles

Versailles is top on the list of what tourists want to see outside of the city. Rapid transit RER line C, with stops all along the left bank of the Seine, will take you there in a jiffy. When you exit at the Versailles station, signs clearly indicate how to walk or take a bus to the château, which is only a short distance away.

The inside of the palace is open daily, except Monday, 9.30–5.30pm, and the vast gardens are open from morning to nightfall. A guided tour of the palace (unaccompanied visits are not allowed) takes about an hour, but you may have to wait in line almost that long beforehand.

It took 50 years to complete Louis XIV's – the Sun King's – plans for this sumptuous palace, a building that gives meaning to the word *grandeur*. In fact, this insensitive display of wealth on the

The grand facade of Versailles

king's part foreshadowed the French Revolution. Because he hated Paris and the unpredictable Parisians, and was jealous of the luxurious castle at Vaux-le-Vicomte built by his finance minister, the young Louis planned his opulent *château* well west of the city. He changed the very landscape to create his gardens, and installed an elaborate system of pumps to bring water from the Seine to his fountains and pools.

More than 1,000 members of court lived in the attic rooms, and life here was as far removed from the life outside the palace walls as they could make it. Such daily events as 'the King's Rise' took on momentous importance for the coterie.

Although revolutionary outrage emptied the castle of most of the furnishings, it has slowly been restored and pieces donated by foreign countries or collected and purchased in France have helped to fill out the many rooms in a style which is approaching the original splendour.

In the precise centre of the palace lie the **Royal Apartments**. The small staircase linking the king's sitting room to the queen's was added by Louis XV and his mistress, Madame de Pompadour. Look for the secret passage later used by Louis XVI's wife, Marie Antoinette, to escape the rabble barging through the gates. That escape is the supposed occasion of her infamous reply to the people's cry for bread: 'Let them eat cake' (*Qu'ils mangent de la brioche*). Historians cast doubt on her actual words, but certainly the sentiment is clear. Poverty and suffering were, perhaps, beyond her imagination, just as the opulence that she took for granted is beyond our own.

The **Hall of Mirrors** was used as a royal reception and ballroom. More recently, the Treaty of Versailles ending World War I was signed here. Another historical event, which the French are less wont to recall, took place here in 1871: the proclamation of the German Empire. The pint-size **Opera House**, built for Louis XV, is a sumptuous hall which once again welcomes special performances, thanks to recent restoration.

Statues everywhere

Outdoors, the park was designed by André le Nôtre, who created the image of the royal garden *à la française*. Three more residences dot the landscape. The **Grand Trianon**, on the bank of the Grand Canal, was built by Louis XIV. He sought peace within its pink marble walls, away from the crowd at court. The **Petit Trianon** was built by his successor, but mainly enjoyed by the last of the Louis, the ill-fated Louis XVI. Queen Marie Antoinette preferred **Le Hameau**, a make-believe hamlet, where she played milkmaid with fine porcelain milk pails.

In the form of a *fleur-de-lys* (symbol of royalty), the **Grand Canal** stretches out from the foot of the terrace, dividing the wooded park in two. The two large fountains in the central alley are the **Latona** and **Apollo** fountains. The first is a weird amphibian allegory dominating the *tapis vert*, the central lawn. The second represents the god driving a chariot led by powerful horses.

Both sides of the park are studded with delightful groves, ponds, exotic bushes, ancient trees and velvety smooth grass. The fountains are so numerous that even a king's coffers couldn't keep them going nowadays, but on the first and third Sundays of June through September, all gush again, their musical splashing joining birdsong. Occasional evening festivities come complete with fireworks and multi-coloured lights. All in all, the fame of this majestic site is well-deserved. As the French saying has it, it is worth the detour.

9. Chartres

Mostly visited for its Gothic cathedral, Chartres is a pleasant and relaxing place to explore. A world away from the big-city mentality of Paris, Chartres is just 60 miles (97 km) southwest, an hour's train ride from Montparnasse station.

The medieval town of Chartres sits upon a plateau hemmed in by wheat fields on the banks of the river Eure. Its **cathedral's** spires rise high above the rich plain, welcoming pilgrims since the 13th century. It is a short walk uphill from the SNCF train station to the site.

View of the cathedral

Extensive restoration work has long kept the cathedral sheathed in scaffolding, but it does not detract from the beauty of the **Rose Windows**. Their fame is due to both beauty and age, for they date from the 12th and 13th centuries, among the oldest examples of this type of religious art to be found in the world. They survived a disastrous fire in 1149 (most of the previous Romanesque cathedral was destroyed), the French Revolution, and two world wars (the windows were removed during World War II).

The 'Chartres blue' in the glass, a rich, deep tone, is not found

In historic Chartres

elsewhere and apparently cannot be duplicated. Some of the panes seem lighter in colour than others, the result of an experimental restoration. Light passing through colours the floor, joining the traces of the ancient marble **Labyrinth** set in the nave. The Labyrinth is symbolic of Christian pilgrimages of the early Middle Ages.

Visit the **Crypt** to see the site of an even more ancient ritual. The cathedral was built on the grounds of a former Druidic worshipping place. You can see a wall of ancient paintings dating from Gallo-Roman times (4th century). Guided tours of the largest and one of the most beautiful crypts in France start from the Maison des Clercs, opposite the south side of the cathedral.

As you leave the cathedral, look up at the two Romanesque towers. The left tower, though known as the 'New Tower', is actually the older, but the delicate Gothic spire atop was added on later, in the 16th century. The thicker spire on the right tower is from the earlier Romanesque period. Here is a good opportunity to observe the difference between these two styles of architecture, both widely present in France.

Behind the cathedral is the **Musée des Beaux Arts**, housing a collection of tapestries, enamels and paintings from the Renaissance through the 18th century. There is also a room devoted to the history of the town. Below the terraced garden behind the museum runs the Eure. It travels past the **Eglise Saint André**, a Romanesque church in poor repair. Follow the pathway along the river, past the traditional wash houses and the remains of the old city wall, all the way to the **Place Saint Pierre**, where another set of magnificent stained-glass windows awaits you in the church.

Most of the old town is a protected site, and has been well-restored and improved with pedestrian areas. It is also a lively agricultural centre and capital of the Beauce region. You can tour the city with an experienced guide. For information and maps, books and brochures, stop in at the tourist office on Rue du Cloître Notre-Dame, right alongside the cathedral.

Rose window, Chartres cathedral

This suggestion for a day trip takes you into Normandy, whose peaceful fields and forests lie just a short distance northwest of Paris. Add adventure to your trip by setting out on a bicycle; SNCF French railways offer rentals right at the station. However you go, take a deep breath of the fragrant countryside.

It's a little more difficult to reach **Giverny** than the previous destinations, but well worth the effort. Take a train from the Gare St Lazare to Vernon, with a journey time of about an hour. At the station, you can take a taxi or hop on a bike for the trip to **Claude Monet's House and Garden** at Giverny. The pink and green house itself is an explosion of colour. The dining room, for example, is bright yellow, lined with priceless chinaware plates. The kitchen is a soaring sky blue. The walls of the artists' rooms are generously hung with Japanese prints from his extensive collection.

The gardens are Monet's paintings come to life – or his paintings are his gardens come to art. Here are the waterlilies, the Japanese bridge, the willow and the pond – so many of the subjects of his Impressionist works.

Not far away is the newly-opened **Musée Américain**, which charts the impact which Monet and the other Impressionists made on American art.

Giverny is very popular on summer afternoons, so start out early on a weekday to get the most pleasure from your visit.

The Seine meets the river Epte here, and there are pretty spots for picnics. If you have a car, continue northwest to **Lyons la Forêt**, a village set in a beech-tree forest. Potted geraniums decorate the windows of typical Normandy half-timbered facades. Otherwise, right in Vernon itself, try the **Restaurant de la Poste**. The fare is simple and inexpensive, and the portions are sized to match hearty country appetites.

Monet's house at Giverny

11. Euro Disney

The Euro Disney Resort, only the second overseas location for Disney outside the US (the other is in Tokyo), opened its doors to the general public in 1992. The site at Marne-la-Vallée is situated 20 miles (32km) east of Paris and can be reached by either car or RER line A from central Paris at Auber, Châtelet or Étoile. Marne-la-Vallée will also be linked up to the high-speed TGV rail network, with direct access to the Channel Tunnel.

Euro Disney's site was chosen because of its centrality to Europe; potential venues in the UK and Spain were discounted because of more difficult access. French reaction to the arrival of Disney was mixed – even though Disney researchers had identified Walt himself as coming originally from the town of Isigny (D'Isigny = Disney).

Huge though the park is, this is only the first stage in its development. In its final form this dream-world will cover an area one-fifth the size of Paris. Visitor figures in its first year easily doubled the number of people going up the Eiffel Tower or visiting the Louvre, but they were lower than Disney had hoped, with the result that some plans are being rescheduled. The park's official language is English, although French is widely spoken.

The gang

Entrance fees vary according to season, but families with children might be better advised spreading their visit over two days. Euro Disney '*passeports*' are available in downtown Paris and at the RER stations. For information and to make reservations in one of the six hotels at Festival Disney – the wider resort – phone (1) 49414010 in Paris, or (71) 753 2900 in London. The on-site hotels can be expensive, although guests have the advantage of earlier access to the site. Restaurants and fast-food outlets are widespread.

Euro Disney is similar in structure to its sister parks in Florida and California. Disney's 'imagineers' have created five imaginary worlds: Fantasyland, Discoveryland, and Main Street USA (representing the early 1900s with ragtime and Dixieland bands), Frontierland and finally Adventureland representing the mysteries of an African-like continent. All are exotically landscaped with a very wide variety of specially-imported trees and plants – many more than in Paris itself – and all are linked by an internal train. The rides and re-creations are of a very high standard and excitement, and 'animatronics' – bringing inanimate objects to life – features highly. In Euro Disney, even queuing can be great entertainment.

Shopping

Duty Free Regulations

US residents may bring back $400 worth of merchandise per traveller for personal use or as gifts, before paying a flat 10 percent tax on additional value up to $1,000. Included in this allowance is 1 litre of alcohol per traveller over age 21 and one bottle of US-trademarked perfume. There is no tax on art or antiques more than 100 years old. Families may pool their declarations, provided that no similar ones have been made in the preceding 30-day period.

Canadian residents have a $300 yearly limit, in addition to the 50 cigars, 200 cigarettes, 2lbs of tobacco and 40oz of alcohol they may bring in tax free.

European Community (EC) countries have an open border policy, which will eventually be accompanied by the standardisation of VAT. Meanwhile, prices (particularly for alcohol and cigarettes) are remarkably different in neighbouring countries. This has resulted in a fair amount of informal import and export, and several UK shopkeepers have taken the opportunity – illegally – to buy produce in French supermarkets for resale in their own outlets in the UK.

Although there is technically no limit on such purchases, consumption has to be for your own personal use. If this is the case, then you may pass through the blue channel at customs and no further tax shall be paid. However, European Community law does set out guidelines as follows: 800 cigarettes, 400 cigarillos, 200 cigars, 1kg of smoking tobacco, 10 litres of spirits, 20 litres of fortified wines, 90 litres of wine, and 110 litres of beer.

Of course, *no animals or pets may be brought into the UK* – and this rule is strictly enforced.

Paris style

Window shopping

Duty free shops, found in the airports and on the planes themselves, are not always the cheapest places to shop. The mark-up (it can be as much as 100 to 200 percent) sometimes overwhelms the tax savings, and you may be better off getting your duty-free goods directly from a shop in town, if you can.

The other alternative is to get the VAT (IVA in France) refunded at the airport. First of all, your purchases in a single store must amount to 1,200 Francs for non-EC residents. The store must fill out a special form (make sure it corresponds to your place of residence). You must include banking information on the form, because refunds are only paid directly into accounts. Customs officials will ask for the forms as you leave, and look at the goods, so allow plenty of time to go through this process.

In general, it is not worth the hassle to seek a refund this way, unless you've got a big item to declare.

Alcohol and Perfumes

If you want to purchase **alcoholic beverages**, I suggest you stick with liqueurs, aperitifs or champagnes. Sadly, a good wine may suffer in the journey and end up disappointing you. Prices of French wines are so competitive around the world that you'd do better to rely on your local supplier. Major supermarkets have the best prices and a satisfactory selection; luxury shops on the Place de la Madeleine offer high-quality items in gift packages.

Perfumes are another favourite, but the prices are only interesting if you are able to purchase them tax-free. This means you should have your plane ticket and passport with you when you go to the shop. Only certain shops offer an instant refund on tax. In addition to Galeries Lafayette and Printemps department stores, two other boutiques in the Opéra district offer this service: **Michel Swiss** and **Raoul & Curly**; the first is right on the Place de l'Opéra (16 Rue de la Paix) and the other is just down the street at 47 Avenue de l'Opéra.

Beauty and Fashion

Fashion is synonymous with Paris, and just looking at Parisians makes you want to dress up. The venerable couture houses are on Avenue Montaigne and Faubourg St Honoré. For less classic and more affordable attire, try around Saint Germain on the Left Bank, or head for the shops of up-and-coming designers Sonia Rykiel or Claude Montana, both on Rue de Grenelle, Nos 6 and 31, respectively (Metro: Saint Sulpice).

Les Halles has a wide selection of clothing inside the Forum shopping centre, or head up nearby Rue du Jour to check out **Agnés B.** and **Gaultier Junior** for a younger look. There are dozens of other shops on this short street selling new and used clothing for men and women.

Keep an eye out for *Soldes*, seasonal sales that usually take place in January and July. *Liquidation* means 'everything must go'. Women's and men's clothes are sized from 36 (small) to 48 (extra large). Shoes start at 36 (English size 5) through 45 (English size 11). Children's clothes are sized by age; baby shoes start at 19. My advice, of course, is to try things on, and any shop will accommodate this request.

To find everyday items that you need while travelling, whether shampoo, a warm sweater, an insole for your shoe, or a sketch pad for your drawings, try one of the many branches of the discount department stores **Monoprix, Uniprix** or **Prisunic**. These stores are very handy, located all over town, smaller and less crowded than the major department stores. Most also offer shoe and clothing repair services and have one floor of grocery items. Clean, inexpensive and well-organised, these stores offer good quality merchandise and are pleasant to shop in.

While you can find many **beauty care products** in these stores, smaller specialised boutiques offer more sophisticated products and perfumes as well as services like manicure, hair removal, facial massage etc in their **Salons de Beauté**. My favourite is **Magic Beauty**, centrally located at 51 Rue de Rivoli. Call 42360635 for an appointment, or just walk in.

Hair dressers are easy enough to locate, but always busy. One of the most popular salons is **Jacques Dessanges**, with 12 locations in the city. Call the Franklin Roosevelt salon on 43593131 for information and an appointment. Another favourite is **Jean Louis David**; he has 14 salons and a beauty school with discount prices on modern styles. Call 43598208. More exclusive is **Maniatis** whose three shops are 18 Rue Marbeuf (Tel: 4723-3014) near the Champs Elysées, 10 Rue Poquelin (Tel: 40289095) in the Forum des Halles, and 35 Rue de Sèvres (Tel: 45441639) near St Germain des Prés.

Fun Souvenirs

The Boutique **Chic et Choc** in Les Halles Metro station takes the cake. They have all sorts of items with the Paris Metro logo. Another special spot is the **Réunion des Musées Nationaux**, 10 Rue de l'Abbaye, near St Germain-des-Prés. They offer posters and catalogues from Paris museums, dating back to 1966, and scarves, handbags and jewellery inspired by the great collections. On a higher price scale, try the **Louvre des Antiquaires**, 2 Place du Palais Royal, for antique furnishings, prints and paintings. Some of the dealers here have less expensive shops elsewhere, so ask for a card.

Adventurous visitors will head for **Flea Markets** to dig out something unique. The most well-known is at the **Porte de Clignancourt**, open only during the weekends (Metro: Porte de Clignancourt). In the city, try the **Marché d'Aligre**, a food and flower market which also has a section of old books, clothes, glassware, lace and jewellery (Place d'Aligre, near Bastille, Metro: Ledru-Rollin; closed Monday). Of the markets outside the city, the best for bargains is the **Marché de Montreuil** to the east (Metro: Porte de Montreuil). Old clothes, junk, and genuine finds all day Saturday, Sunday and Monday.

A few other suggestions for take-homes that you can pick up and pack easily: perfumed soaps in decorative boxes (look in the pharmacy windows); chocolates and other sweet-meats in pretty packets, sold in bakeries and *confiseries*, mustard and vinegar assortments in attractive jars and bottles; 'Perfumes of Paris' collections with sample sizes of an assortment of scents, on sale in many of the smaller beauty product boutiques.

The only problem with shopping in Paris is trying to decide how much you can spend. But even Uncle Scrooge could cough up for a pair of Eiffel Tower earrings (10 to 50 Francs in souvenir shops) or a sachet of lavender to perfume the linen closet (10 to 30 Francs, in department stores or from street vendors).

Preparing for a closer look

PATISSERIE
GARANTIE PUR BEURRE

Eating Out

It would take years to sample all the restaurants in Paris, and a staff to keep up with changes and openings. Parisians enjoy eating out of their favourite *bistro* as much as discovering a new restaurant or having a night out in a really fine establishment. Take the suggestions given in each itinerary in this book, or walk into a place that looks (and smells) great, or just try the restaurants listed below. Addresses include the *code postale*, of which the last two numbers indicate the district (*arrondissement*). Prices are based on the set price menu, if there is one, or a three-course *à la carte* meal for one person, with a moderately-priced wine.

Many restaurants close on Sunday. Reservations are required in expensive restaurants, and highly recommended on Friday and Saturday nights for moderate restaurants.

The price of dinner may vary, especially if you order a special bottle of wine or champagne. Lunch is served from noon until about 2pm. Dinner service starts around 8pm. *Brasseries* serve a limited menu (eggs, hot ham sandwiches, sausages) all day; cafés generally have cold sandwiches on crusty *baguettes* of bread at any hour. If you want a super gourmet experience, try lunchtime, rather than dinner, when many expensive places have set menus that can offer real savings over *à la carte*.

One of the joys of Paris

Expensive Restaurants

Dinner with a moderately-priced wine costs at least 500 Francs per person. Lunch is much cheaper, especially for set menus.

LA TOUR D'ARGENT
15 Quai de la Tournelle (75005)
Tel: 43542331
Closed on Monday, credit cards: American Express, Diner's Club and Visa
Famous for the view of Notre Dame as well as recipes based on duck. The service is impeccable, the décor divine. Dinner, minimum 900 Francs.

LASERRE
17 Ave Franklin Roosevelt (75008)
Tel: 43595343
Closed on Sunday, Monday and in August, no credit cards accepted
In the summer, you dine under the stars when they roll back the ceiling upstairs. Incredible wine list, dishes rather on the delicate side. Just using the extravagant cutlery is half the pleasure. Around 700 Francs.

CHEZ JAMIN
32 Rue de Longchamp (75016)
Tel: 47271227
Closed on weekends, and in July, credit cards: American Express, Diner's Club and Visa

Dress up for this one

A gastronomic *ne plus ultra*, specialising in *nouvelle cuisine*. Reservations are accepted eight weeks in advance! The menu is about 980 Francs, excluding wine, per person.

ARPEGE
84 Rue de Varenne (75007)
Tel: 45514733 and 45512002
Closed Saturday, Sunday lunch, and end of July until 21 August, credit cards: American Express, Diner's Club and Visa
This superb restaurant is among the top 12 in Paris. The wine-cellar is particularly good, and not expensive. Between 500 and 900 Francs, excluding wine.

There's good food everywhere

Moderate Restaurants

There is an abundance of restaurants in this category, where a meal for one with wine costs between 150 and 300 Francs. Here are a few favourites that are not included in the itineraries:

TERMINUS NORD
23 Rue de Dunkerque (75010)
Tel: 42850515
Open daily, credit cards: American Express, Diner's Club and Visa
Just across from the *Gare du Nord* station, this big, busy brasserie has a 1925 décor and a staff of very professional waiters. Hearty portions for healthy appetites, traditional French food including seafood specials, excellent beef and lamb dishes.

Look for the specials

LE BAR DES THÉATRES
6 Ave Montaigne (75008)
Tel: 47233463
Open daily, credit card: Visa
This busy, noisy place has been around for 40 years, serving tasty and traditional French food in a friendly atmosphere. Don't mind the napkins, and keep away if you hate cigarette smoke – but this place typifies the kind of restaurant that used to make people say it was just about impossible to get a bad meal in France.

AUBERGE DE JARENTE
7 Rue de Jarente (75004)
Tel: 43547806
Closed Sunday, Monday and in August, credit cards: American Express, Diner's Club and Visa
Small welcoming restaurant specialising in Basque dishes. The uncomplicated cuisine makes a welcome change from some French establishments. Try the *piperade de St Jean* and *gâteau Basque*.

LA CITROUILLE
10 Rue Grégoire de Tours (75006)
Tel: 43299041 Open daily
In the heart of the Latin Quarter near Odéon, the restaurant serves fresh salads and simple well-prepared dishes at low prices – a nice escape from steak and French fries!

LE POETE IVRE
8 Rue Leopold (75002)
Tel: 40262646
Closed Sunday, credit cards: Visa

One of the best Thai restaurants in town. It is quite small but well known so you should book if you plan to eat there on a Friday or Saturday. Situated in an old and quiet part of Paris.

NOS ANCETRES LES GAULOIS
39 Rue Saint Louis en l'Ille (75004)
Tel: 46336607
Open nightly, credit cards: CB, Diner's Club and Visa
On the chic island of St Louis right in the centre of town, Nos Ancêtres has a reputation for being unique which is based more on the ambience than the food. The menu mainly offers grilled meats and the hearty portions are served with strong wine by Gaulish characters in winged helmets. Good value and good fun.

CHEZ MA COUSINE
12 Rue Norvins (75018)
Tel: 46064935
Open daily, credit cards: American Express, Diner's Club, Mastercard and Visa
In Montmartre, right on the Place du Tertre, this small and friendly place also offers a cabaret in the evening, and has a *crêpe* stand on the street.

Inexpensive Restaurants
For around 150 Francs a person, you can have the pleasure of a good French meal and wine at the following:

CHARTIER
7 Rue du Faubourg Montmartre (75009)
Tel: 47708629 Closed Sunday
Near the Opéra, the best-known low-price eatery in town. The ambience is an experience in itself: turn-of-the-century decor, snappy waiters, shared tables and plenty of *bonhommie*. Arrive before 2pm in the afternoon or 9.30 at night, or you probably won't get a seat.

POLIDOR
41 Rue Monsieur-le-Prince (75006)
Closed on Sunday, Monday and in August
Favoured by students and professors, this Latin Quarter hangout offers home-style cooking and art-deco design. Everything is very relaxed, including the service, and no gastronomic miracles are in order, but Hemingway ate here, and so can you.

LE LAZARE
68 Rue Quincampoix 75003
Open evenings from 7–12.30am
Closed Sunday and Monday
M. Toyre, the current owner of this mellow restaurant, was born in the same year that his parents opened their establishment. His wife now works at the stove, cooking up hearty French dishes (the four-course menu with wine is just 105 Francs) and a *bouillabaisse* special (175 Francs including wine). Very quiet and friendly, this lovely place has weathered the neighbourhood's many changes with dignity and charm.

PASTAVINO
6 Rue Pierre Lescot (75001)
59 Rue Dauphine (75006)
and 30 Rue Passy (75016)
One branch inside the Forum des Halles shopping centre; one on the street leading off the Pont Neuf at the tip of the Ile de la Cité; and one in the 16th. This Italian restaurant and take-away serves salads, pasta dishes and tasty desserts at unbeatable prices.

Bars and Wine Bars
LE RUBIS
10 Rue du Marché St Honoré (75001)
Closed on weekends and in August
This is the place to be when the *Beaujolais Nouveau* comes out in October, and the party fills up the whole street.

In other seasons, it is a nice place for lunch and to have a glass of something divine.

L'ECLUSE
15 Quai des Grands-Augustins (75006), Rue Mondétour (75001), Rue du Pont Lodi (75006), Place de la Madeleine (75008), Rue François 1er (75008). All branches are closed on Sunday
The grand-daddy of Parisian wine bars. Rather expensive, but an outstanding selection of Bordeaux wines by the glass or bottle, and an appetising choice of simple foods to accompany them.

HARRY'S BAR
5 Rue Daunou (75002)
I couldn't leave this one out – famous around the world, Harry's opened in 1911, was second home to Hemingway (as were many bars in Paris!), and the Bloody Mary was created here. Still popular and plenty of characters to check out until the wee early hours.

Drink in the sun

Nightlife

There is plenty to do in Paris after the street-lights blink on. Expect a late start in summer.

River tours: The **Vedettes du Pont Neuf**, entrance under the bridge near St Michel and Notre Dame, leave roughly every 30 minutes until 5pm Monday to Thursday, and until 10pm the rest of the week. The trip takes about an hour and powerful spotlights illuminate the bridges and buildings as you go. The same tours are run by **Bateaux Mouches** at Pont d'Alma, although less frequently. Across from the Eiffel Tower at the Pont d'Iéna are **Les Bateaux Parisiens**, who also offer gastronomic cruises.

Nocturnal bus tours: These pass the spendidly illuminated monuments of the city. Some end at the Moulin Rouge for French can-can and champagne, or the Lido on the Champs-Elysées. Two well-known tours in town are **Paris Vision** (214 Rue de Rivoli 75001) and **Cityrama** (4 Place des Pyramides 75001); their packages are also sold in many agencies, and most hotels carry their leaflets. The companies also organise day trips outside town to popular sites such as Versailles, Giverny, Euro Disney and Chartres.

Stage: Tickets to the ballet, opera, concerts, or theatre productions can be bought at an agency or at the theatre itself. The FNAC stores (music and books) around town (there's a main branch in the Forum des Halles shopping centre) sell tickets to most concerts. For theatrical productions, go to the Kiosque de la Madeleine, a big ticket booth in the middle of Place de la Madeleine. You can buy half-price tickets on the day.

Complete weekly listings are in *L'Officiel des Spectacles* and other magazines. Also look out for Paris's distinctive green 'Morris Columns', on street corners, which are usually splashed with posters.

See Paris by night

Late night sounds

Jazz clubs

Paris loves jazz and clubs seem to have undergone a renaissance recently. Check the *L'Officiel des Spectacles* to see what's on in the following clubs:

NEW MORNING
7–9 Rue des Petits Ecuries (75010)
Big, scant décor, tucked in a back alley. Good acoustics. Some greats keep coming back, including Richie Havens, Taj Mahal, Wayne Shorter, Stan Getz and Prince. Very informal and hip, for serious music lovers.

BAR LIONEL HAMPTON
Hotel Meridian
81 Blvd Gouvion-St Cyr (75017)
A favourite with performers and fans. Seats several hundred. Run by a local jazz hero known simply as Moustache, who shows some of the finest jazz musicians, such as Harry Edison, Oscar Peterson, Memphis Slim and Benny Carter the respect they deserve. Not a night owl? Enjoy jazz here on Sunday, over brunch.

LE PETIT JOURNAL
71 Blvd St Michel (75005) and
LE PETIT JOURNAL MONTPARNASSE
13 Rue du Commandant-Mouchotte (75014)
Same owners, different styles. The first features Dixieland and Swing, the second contemporary names like Herbie Hancock, Art Blakey and

Stéphane Grappelli. Both good food and good vibes.

After-Hours Clubs

Clubs in Paris tend to be very 'clubby' subjecting would-be partiers to heavy scrutiny at the door. No grubby clothes, so dress fashionably, and don't forget to bring plenty of money. For all sorts of adventures:

LES BAINS
7 Rue du Bourg-l'Abbé (75003)
Old public bath house, the gathering place of fashion victims and the young and hip. To be sure of getting in, make a reservation to eat at the restaurant first (Tel: 48870180).

LE TANGO
13 Rue au Maire (75003)
A meeting place for African *sapeurs*, guys who spend fantastic sums of money on incredible-looking clothes. A wild time in store, if you're dressed right!

LE GARAGE
41 Rue Washington (75008)
Not far from the Champs Elysées. A little more low-key. Current hits and retro music, a light show. A favourite of more mature customers.

A night out

Calendar of Special Events

The main tourist season in Paris is from June through September, and Easter is also a very busy period. July and August are big holiday months for the French, so a number of shops, restaurants and theatres are closed. However, there is still plenty for visitors to do, including summer festivals, sound and light shows, and fireworks displays, and there is a happy and relaxed atmosphere in the city streets, which are less crowded than at other times of the year.

National holidays involve bank closings and heavy traffic, so plan around the following: **1 January, Easter Monday, 1 May (Labour Day), 8 May (VE Day), Pentecost (Whit Monday), 14 July, 15 August (Assumption), 1 November (All Saints' Day), 11 November (Armistice), 25 December.**

When packing seasonable clothes for your holiday, keep in mind that the French, and especially Parisians, dress up to go to work, out to dinner, or to the theatre. Jeans are fine for visiting museums, but frowned upon in many restaurants and shops.

The Tour de France passes through

National colours on Bastille Day

JANUARY–MARCH

The weather is cold and damp, and the only advantages at this time are the lower fares and hotel rates, and the absence of crowds at museums and monuments.

APRIL–MAY

Springtime in Paris is a legend, of course, and one the city usually lives up to, if for a fleeting moment. Temperatures range from 60–70°F (16–22°C). The days lengthen deliciously as heavy chestnut blooms appear against the unfurling green foliage. If you are lucky with your timing, Paris in these months is at its most intoxicating.

JUNE–JULY

In the early part of the summer there are many celebrations. The Festival du Marais goes on for two months, presenting concerts, theatre and dance in some of the neighbourhood's lovely old buildings and churches, as well as special events held in major halls. This more than makes up for annual closings. On 21 June is the Fête de la Musique, held on the longest day of the year right into the morning. There are free concerts at outdoor bandstands set up around the city as well as spontaneous events.

The Tour de France bicycle race sprints to a finish on the Champs Elysées around 14 July. That is timed to coincide with Bastille Day, known in France as La Fête Nationale. The party is in the streets, starting with the morning military parade down the Champs Elysées, through fireworks over the Eiffel Tower, and dancing till dawn at the numerous Firemen's Balls. Watch out for sizzling firecrackers!

AUGUST

The city slows down in August and you can enjoy the holiday atmosphere. Visit the fair in the Tuileries Park and go on the big Ferris wheel for a thrilling view.

SEPTEMBER

This is an excellent month for visiting, known as *la rentrée*, or the return. New fashions, plays, and a major art show, the Foire Internationale de l'Art Contemporain (FIAC).

OCTOBER–NOVEMBER

October is wine month, with the Montmartre harvest festival and the arrival of Beaujolais Nouveau. It is also time for the International Dance Festival, which continues through November.

DECEMBER

Christmas starts in the shops around the end of November, and the streets are magnificent to see. The days are short and cold, but the city has a bustling, busy quality in the days preceding the end-of-the-year holidays. Christmas is celebrated in the family for the most part, while New Year's Eve is a big party occasion.

Practical information

GETTING THERE

You could arrive at one of two airports serving Paris. Charles de Gaulle (also referred to as 'Roissy') is bigger and more modern. You can take a comfortable and inexpensive Air France bus to the Arc de Triomphe, then take a bus, the Metro or a cab to your hotel. There are also city buses (Nos 350 and 351) which go into Eastern Paris, Nation and the Gare de l'Est train station. A taxi takes about 40 to 50 minutes to reach the centre, and costs about 220 Francs. Add another 30 minutes for rush hours.

Orly is the other major airport, which handles mostly domestic flights and char-

ters. Air France buses go to the Invalides Terminal, a convenient drop-off place, where you can board the Metro or RER directly. A city bus ('Orlybus') comes into the southern end of Paris at the Denfert-Rochereau Metro station every 15 minutes. A taxi ride, not during rush hour, takes 30-40 minutes and costs about 150 Francs.

If you arrive at a train station, you can follow the clearly posted signs towards the Metro or taxi stands.

TRAVEL ESSENTIALS

Visas

Travellers to France must have a valid passport. Visitors from EC countries and America do not need visas, but visitors from other countries should contact the nearest French consulate or their local tourist office about obtaining one before travelling.

Time

France is six hours ahead of US Eastern Standard time and two hours ahead of Greenwich Mean Time.

Electricity

Paris runs on 220 volts, 50 cycles, although there are still a few older buildings on 110. Devices marked 220/240 volts will work in Paris, but not at top

Gare St Lazarre

speed. If you carry a travel iron or hair dryer, for example, make sure you have an adaptor so that it will fit in the French socket. If you've forgotten to bring one along, you can buy one from an 'Electricité' or 'Quincaillerie' (hardware) shop.

Cash supplier

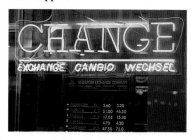

MONEY MATTERS

Many banks in Paris will change cash or travellers' cheques, and there are no special differences in rates. Banking hours are 9am–4.30pm on weekdays. The exchange window at the Gare du Nord is open until 10pm on weekdays, and other station banks are open until 8pm.

There are automatic exchange machines at the Opéra (the BNP Bank) and at No 66 on the Champs Elysées (BRED) that will convert other bills into Francs. International Visa cards can be used in automatic tellers at many city banks. The exchange bureaux in downtown areas often offer rather poor rates – or else a high commission. Either way you'd do better with a bank.

Hotline numbers for lost cards: American Express (Tel: 47777200); Diners Club (Tel: 47627575); Carte Bleu/Visa (Tel: 42771190).

The basic unit of money is the Franc, divided into 100 Centimes. Coin units are used for 5, 10, 20 and 50 Centimes; 1, 2, 5 and 10 Francs. In circulation are the bills for 20, 50, 100, 200 and 500 Francs.

A few sample costs in Paris: movie tickets, 30–40 Francs; theatre 100+ Francs; glass of wine in a café 10–20 Francs; soft drink 15+ Francs; tea 20 Francs; pastry in a bakery 10–15 Francs; pastry in a café 20–30 Francs; cigarettes 10–15 Francs a pack; foreign newspapers 12+ Francs.

Tipping

Common in a number of situations; in hotels, restaurants and cafés, a service charge is always included. However, people usually leave something in the saucer, often the small change returned from the bill. Prices may be listed *prix nets* or *service compris*, in which case, service is included in the price. If the price says *service en sus* or *service non compris*, you can expect an extra 12 or 15 percent to be added to the total.

A tip of 5 Francs is usually given to: room service waiters (except breakfast), ushers, washroom attendants, hat check clerks. Taxi drivers and hairdressers expect about 15 percent.

GETTING AROUND

Paris is divided into 20 *arrondissements* (districts) which spiral out from the Louvre Palace in a snail-shell pattern. The last numbers of the postal code beginning with 750- are the *arrondissement* number. Handy book-format street maps are on sale in most café-tabacs, news stands and many bookstores. While in the Metro, ask for a free map (*un plan du Métro*) and a copy of the public transportation guide *Paris Patchwork*.

The Metro

Metro, Buses and Trains

You can travel on bus and Metro with tickets purchased at the ticket booth in any Metro station. These are much cheaper when you buy ten at once (*un carnet*). There is a tourist card called *Paris Visite*, available for foreign visitors and valid for three to five days of unlimited travel on the Metro, bus (including airports), and suburban SNCF lines.

The one-day card is called *Formule 1*.

It gives discounts on certain boat tours, the Montparnasse Tower, and SNCF bicycle rental at Compiègne or Vernon (among other stations).

It is very simple to use the **Metro** system, which is the densest in the world with stops an average of every 55 metres (180ft). The lines are named after their terminal points, for example Château de Vincennes-Pont de Neuilly crosses the city from east to west, ending at those two stops. You can transfer as many times as you need to on the same ticket, by following the orange signs marked *Correspondances* in the tunnels.

There are big maps in every station to guide you. In general, the Metro is quite safe, although you must watch out for your wallet, especially when surrounded by big crowds.

Trains run from 5.30am–12.30am every day. Follow the sign *Accés aux Quais* to reach the tracks, and *Sortie* to get out to the street. Keep a hold of your ticket until you exit the system: it may be checked by inspectors.

Buses run on different schedules, but usually start around 7am and stop around 8.45pm. Only certain buses run on Sunday or late at night. Bus shelters all have maps and route information, and if you board a bus you must show your pass or punch a ticket in the machine next to the driver. Look at the route map to see how many bus zones you'll be going through, if more than two, you must punch two tickets; except for the Petite Ceinture, a bus service which circles the boundaries of Paris. You would need to use up to five tickets to complete the round.

If you're good at deciphering public transport systems, the city buses are really a great way to get around, even though they are admittedly not as fast as the Metro. At least you see Paris from the buses.

The RER lines are rapid transit lines that go out to the suburbs. They can be useful for crossing town quickly, and you can use a Metro ticket on the RER within the city. But to get to Versailles, for example, if you don't have a pass that covers it, you must buy a more expensive ticket, which you will have to insert in a machine in order to exit the station on arrival.

Taxis

Taxis are best found at taxi stands, clearly marked by large signs. You can also call a taxi company. Alpha Taxi (Tel: 45858585); Taxi Bleu: (Tel: 42024202). Both offer 24-hour service. If you call a taxi, the meter starts running when the driver gets the call. There is an extra charge for luggage, train-station pick-up, and sometimes authorised rate hikes may be posted in the window. Three passengers is the limit, and cabbies are strict about this rule.

I do not recommend renting a car to visit Paris. Driving conditions are difficult and you really have no need to suffer traffic jams.

HOURS AND HOLIDAYS

Banks have various hours (see *Money Matters*), generally from 9am–4.30pm Monday to Friday, with some branches closed at lunchtime, and/or on Monday; some open on Saturday until noon.

The **Post Office** is open daily from 9am–6pm and Saturday until noon (for branches with longer hours, see *Communications and News* in this chapter.)

Department stores are open from 10am–6.30pm, and normally close on Sunday. Many smaller shops close on Monday (especially food stores) and some on Wednesday. Bakeries and some others

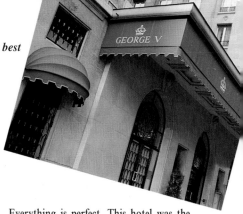
One of the best

close for lunch from about 1–4pm. Most shops open until 7–8pm.

Public offices are open from 9am–5pm Monday to Friday, and sometimes on Saturday morning, and are often closed for two hours from noon–2pm.

ACCOMMODATION

Although there are many, many hotels in Paris, due to the steady stream of visitors – not just seasonal tourists but also visitors to trade fairs, congresses and the like – it can be hard to find a room. Your travel agent will probably offer to book a room for you, which is a good idea. Otherwise, it is wise to reserve in advance. If you haven't done so, you can save foot-work by checking with the Tourist Office on the Champs Elysées (Metro: Charles de Gaulle) or in any of the train stations. They charge a small fee for finding a room. You can also call or write to the hotels listed below to make a reservation. In that case, be prepared to send a deposit ahead of you. Your choice ranges from the deluxe to the merely adequate. Here are a few suggestions at different rates. Breakfast is usually extra, starting at about 30 Francs.

Deluxe Hotels

A double room with a bath costs about 1,700 Francs a night.

INTERCONTINENTAL PARIS
3 Rue de Castiglione (75001)
Tel: 42603780, credit cards: American Express, Diners, Mastercard and Visa.
460 rooms, excellent location, great service, all modern conveniences including air conditioning.

MEURICE
228 Rue de Rivoli (75001)
Tel: 42603806, credit cards: American Express, Diners, Mastercard and Visa.
161 rooms, modern conveniences in a lovely old building, air conditioning.

RITZ
15 Place Vendôme (75001)
Tel: 42603830, credit cards: American Express, Diners, Mastercard and Visa.

Everything is perfect. This hotel was the inspiration for the word 'ritzy'. 164 rooms, good restaurants, spacious public rooms, all conveniences, air conditioning and secretarial services.

CRILLON
10 Place de la Concorde (75008)
Tel: 42669145, credit cards: American Express, Diners, Mastercard and Visa.
191 rooms, fantastic site with some views over the river, next door to the American Embassy. Refurbished in the early 1980s, excellent restaurant, air conditioning.

PLAZA-ATHÉNÉE
25 Ave Montaigne (75008)
Tel: 47237833, credit cards: American Express, Diners, Mastercard and Visa.
218 sound-proofed rooms and suites near the Champs Elysées. Restaurants, disco, air conditioning.

GEORGE V
31 Ave George V (75008)
Tel: 47235400, credit cards: American Express, Diners, Mastercard and Visa.
292 rooms, completely modern and air conditioned. The restaurant and bar are very popular with the international upper-crust, including starlets, film agents and businessmen.

Expensive Hotels

For a double room with a bath, expect to pay about 600 to 900 Francs.

NORMANDY
7 Rue de l'Echelle (75001)
Tel: 42603021, credit cards: American Express, Diners, Mastercard and Visa.
138 rooms, most with bathrooms. Restaurant and bar. Comfortable and relaxing.

DEUX-ILES
59 Rue St Louis-en-L'Ile (75004)
Tel: 43261335
17 rooms, all with bath or shower in a lovely 17th-century house; peaceful and friendly; bar and sitting room.

ANGLETERRE
44 Rue Jacob (75006)
Tel: 42603472, credit cards: American Express, Diners and Visa.
30 rooms, all with bath or shower, in what was once the home of the British Ambassador. Good service, traditional surroundings, central location.

HOLIDAY INN
69 Blvd Victor (75015)
Tel: 45337463 and
10 Place de la République (75010)
Tel: 43554434
The first has 90 rooms with baths, near the Porte de Versailles exhibition centre. The second, 333 rooms, all with bath or shower. Both have a restaurant, bar, air conditioning.

TERRASSE
12–14 Rue Joseph-de-Maistre (75018)
Tel: 46067285, credit cards: American Express, Diners, Mastercard and Visa.
108 rooms in Montmartre, baths. Restaurant and bar, calm location.

Moderate Hotels

One night in a double hotel room of this category costs about 250–500 Francs. All of the below have fewer than 100 rooms, some with bath/shower rooms and some without.

TIMHOTEL
This new, moderately priced chain has several hotels in town, all well fitted (all rooms with bath) and small and friendly. All are recommended highly and definitely require reservations. Here are their locations:

ITALIE
22 Rue Barrault (75013)

TOLBIAC
35 Rue Tolbiac (75013)

MONTMARTRE
11 Place Emile Goudeau (75018)

MONTPARNASSE
22 Rue de l'Arrivée (75015)

LE LOUVRE
4 Rue Croix des Petits Champs (75001)

LA BOURSE
3 Rue de la Banque (75002)

SAINT LAZARE
113 Rue St Lazare (75008)

Call the central reservation service to book a room: Tel: 42962828. *Credit Cards: American Express, Diners, Mastercard and Visa.*

GRANDES ECOLES
75 Rue du Cardinal Lemoine (75005)
Tel: 43267923
Not very fancy, but well-located and pleasant, good value.

ST JACQUES
35 Rue des Ecoles (75005)
Tel: 43268253
Like the above, an ordinary Parisian hotel, centrally located.

HOTEL D'AGUESSEAU
24 Rue Boissy d'Anglas (75008)
Tel: 42659120
Beautiful location, very friendly staff and cosy rooms, good value.

Inexpensive Hotels

This category includes hotels under 250 or 300 Francs, of which there are many in Paris, particularly around the railway stations. The rooms provide minimal but adequate comfort. There may be a big difference in price between rooms with and without private bath/shower/toilet. Breakfast optional.

PALAIS
2 Quai de la Mégisserie (75001)
Tel: 42369825
19 rooms near the Sainte Chapelle, some with bathrooms.

ESMERALDA
4 Rue St Julien le Pauvre (75002)
Tel: 43541920
19 rooms (16 with bath/shower) near Notre Dame in the busy Latin Quarter.

PLACE DES VOSGES
12 Rue Birague (75004)
Tel: 42726046, credit cards: American Express, Diners, Mastercard and Visa.
16 rooms, all with bath or shower, Marais district. Very pleasant, small and friendly – book well in advance!

VIEUX PARIS
9 Rue Gît-le-Coeur (75006)
Tel: 43544166
21 rooms, 14 with bath or showers, near the river and St Michel. Quaint, albeit slightly frayed furnishings.

PALAIS BOURBON
49 Rue de Bourgogne (75007)
Tel: 47052926
26 rooms with bath/shower and 8 others without. Small but modern, has a bar. Quiet, distinguished neighbourhood of government ministries, the Invalides and the Rodin Museum.

Ask a policeman

HEALTH AND EMERGENCIES

If you lose your money, passport or other papers, or if they are stolen, look for the police station (*Commissariat*) nearest the site of theft or loss to make an official declaration before reporting to the embassy of your country.

Police Emergency
Tel: 17

Fire Department
Tel: 18 (emergency first aid)

Doctor
SOS Médecins
Tel: 43377777 or 47077777

American Hospital
Tel: 47475300

British Hospital
Tel: 47581312

British and American Pharmacy
1 Rue Auber (75009)
Metro: Opéra
8.30am–8pm Monday to Saturday, English spoken.

Pharmacie Anglo-Américaine
6 Rue Castiglione (75001)
Metro: Tuileries
9am–7.30pm Monday to Saturday, English spoken.

SOS-Help
English spoken
Crisis hot line: 47238080 from 3–11 pm (subject to change).

COMMUNICATIONS AND NEWS

Post Offices

Post offices are open from 8am–6pm Monday to Friday, and some are open until noon on Saturday. You can spot them by the yellow sign with a bird silhouette and the letters PTT. There are two branches with extended hours. Poste Louvre (52 Rue du Louvre, 75001, Metro: Louvre or Les Halles); 8am–midnight Sunday to Thursday and 24 hours on Friday, Saturday and the 14th and 15th of each month. Poste Paris 8 (71 Ave des Champs Elysées, 75008, Metro: Franklin Roosevelt), open from 8am–11pm, Monday to Friday.

Telephones and Telegrams

Public telephones can be found in all post offices; there are booths on the street; a café-tabac has a telephone and most ordinary cafés have phones for the use of customers. In cafés, you may have to buy a token (*jeton*) at the counter, or pay the cashier directly, or use a coin in the phone. Otherwise, most public phones now take *Télécartes*, plastic cards, which are sold in denominations of 50 units upwards. They are useful for local and international calls; a flashing panel tells you how much time you have left.

To call other countries, first dial the access code **19**: **Australia** (61); **Germany** (49); **Italy** (39); **Netherlands** (31); **Spain** (34); **UK** (44); **US** and **Canada** (1). If using a US credit phone card, call the company's access number below: AT&T, Tel: 078 11-0010; MCI, Tel: 078 11-0012; Sprint, Tel: 078 11-0014.

Telegrams can be sent from any Post Office. There is a special phone number for telegrams in English: 42332111. **Telefax** services are available at the Louvre Post Office (address above) and at a few branches. There is a Telex service at 7 Rue Feydeau (75002), open from 8am–8pm, Metro: Bourse.

Media and Bookstores

To keep on top of what is happening while you are in town, the *L'Officiel des Spectacles* publishes an extensive list of restaurants, bars and clubs, concerts, plays and movies in town, information on museums, tours and sports, with hours, addresses and phone numbers. Similar and equally good magazines are *Sept à Paris* and *Pariscope*.

In English, *Passion* magazine is a big-format monthly with restaurant and film reviews, calendar of events, and a summer supplement mini-guide. You can find these three publications at any news stand.

American and British papers and magazines are available at many news stands too. For further English reading, try these big bookshops:

BRENTANO'S
37 Ave de l'Opéra (75002)
Metro: Opéra

GALIGNANI
224 Rue de Rivoli (75001)
Metro: Tuileries

SHAKESPEARE & CO
37 Rue de la Bûcherie (75005)
Metro: St Michel

W H SMITH
248 Rue de Rivoli (75001)
Metro: Concorde

MUSEUMS

The museums of Paris deserve every bit of the praise lavished upon them by visitors from near and far. Check the *Officiel* magazine for ongoing exhibitions and precise information on opening hours (these are subject to change). City of Paris museums close on Monday, national museums on Tuesday, and private museums may close on Tuesday or Friday. Admission charges vary, but 30 Francs is about the average for one adult entrance. There are reductions for students, chil-

LA POSTE

PARIS
CHAMPS ÉLYSÉES

dren under 18, and seniors, so bring along identification if you fit any of these categories. Many national museums are free or half-priced on Sunday. The **Carte Musées** (available in main Metro stations, museums and monuments) gives you access to over 60 museums and monuments in Paris (including the Louvre, Orsay, Pompidou, Picasso, La Villette, Versailles, Notre Dame...) for a period of 1, 3 or 5 days.

In addition to the museums included in the itineraries in this book, there are many others well worth a visit. Here are a few:

MUSÉE DES ARTS DÉCORATIFS
107-109 Rue de Rivoli (75001)
Metro: Palais Royal
Open 12.30–6pm Wednesday to Sunday. This recently renovated museum is heaven for interior decorators. Beautifully crafted furniture, shiny porcelain and crystal, gleaming silver and gold objects as well as statues and paintings.

MUSÉE D'ORSAY
1 Rue de Bellechasse (75007)
Metro: Solférino; RER: Orsay
Open 10am–6pm, Thursday until 9.15pm (tickets sold until 8pm). Closed on Tuesday. The vast, long-abandoned Orsay train station in the centre of town was saved from destruction many years ago, but not until recently did it discover its new vocation.

Preserving the building's *belle époque* architecture, Gae Aulenti redesigned the inner space into several exhibition levels, while keeping all the open, airy majesty of the original train station.

Now it is devoted to works from the last half of the 19th century. One section, showing works by Delacroix and Ingres, leads up to the birth of Impressionism in the 1870s. Witness the changing aesthetics in works by Monet, Manet and Renoir. On the upper level, there are numerous works by Van Gogh and Cézanne. A good part of the collection is from the old Jeu de Paume Museum (the latter is now reserved for special shows).

Exhibitions in the two towers bring us up to the end of the century with sleek Art Nouveau. Between them, a platform and a giant transparent clock provide a pretty view across the Seine river to the gardens of the Louvre. You can rest and refresh yourself at the restaurant/café on this level.

MUSÉE GREVIN (Waxworks)
10 Blvd Montmartre (75009)
and 'Grand Balcon' in the Forum des Halles shopping centre
The first (Metro: Rue Montmartre) is open daily from 1–7pm (last tickets sold at 6pm). The second (Metro: Les Halles) is open from 10.20am–7.30pm on weekdays, and from 1–8pm on Sunday and holidays. Plenty of turn-of-the-century characters and a few present-day stars animate the museums, which are very popular with children.

MUSÉE D'ART MODERNE DE LA VILLE DE PARIS
11 Ave du Président Wilson (75016)
Metro: Alma-Marceau, Iéna
Open 10am–5pm, Wednesday until 8.30pm. Closed on Monday. Somewhat neglected, overshadowed by many other new museums in recent years, this big, echoing place is usually calm, cool and uncrowded on a summer day, a good place to seek relief from the crowds and the elements. The period of art represented here falls somewhere between Orsay and the Pompidou Centre, Post Impressionism up through Braque and Rouault. One wing now houses the **Musée d'Art et**

Disabled

Disabled travellers will have difficulty using public transport and access to many older buildings is limited. Some efforts are made however, and there is a taxi service for people in wheelchairs, special bus service for the disabled, and the Louvre museum offers tours for handicapped (including blind) individuals.

The government publishes a booklet, *Touristes quand même*, which you can order or pick up in person at the French National Tourist Office, Parisian tourist offices, or directly from the Comité National Français de Liaison pour la Réadaptation des Handicapés, 38 Blvd Raspail (75007).

Senior Citizens and Families

Seniors in Paris can benefit from many reductions and advantages after age 60 or 65. In order to do so, you of course must provide proof of age, and in some cases (for reduced train fares, for example) you must provide a passport-sized photo which is affixed to a discount card.

A reduction for families together (*Familles nombreuses*) is applied in some museums and for train fares at off-peak periods.

Tourist Offices

The main Tourist Office for Paris is at 127 Avenue des Champs Elysées (75008), Metro: Charles de Gaulle-Etoile. It is often crowded, but the staff do a good job providing information in English, book-

d'Essai (closed on Tuesday). Also known as the *Palais de Tokyo*, the space is used for changing exhibits.

USEFUL INFORMATION

Children

For children, there are several baby-sitting services available in town; I suggest Kid Service (Tel: 429601016). Museums that are specially interesting to young travellers are Orsay (interactive computer terminals), Musée de la Marine, La Villette. There is a very good children's library in the Pompidou Centre, where older kids can amuse themselves while big folks tour the museum.

Kids who are old enough can also be left in the Jardin des Halles play area at the Forum des Halles while you shop. There are puppet theatres in the Luxembourg Gardens, in the Champs de Mars park next to the Eiffel Tower, and at the Rond Point des Champs Elysées in the grassy parkland at the bottom of the Avenue of the same name.

Students

Students must bring a valid student ID with a photo in order to get reductions at museums, theatres, and for concerts. You can get more information on what's available at the Council on International Educational Exchange, 1 Place de l'Odéon (75006).

Another useful address for young travellers is the *Accueil des Jeunes en France*, 119 Rue St Martin (75004), Metro: Rambuteau. They can help with budget lodging and information on activities where you can meet people.

…and luggage

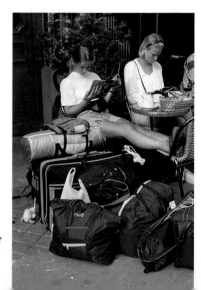

ing hotels or travel arrangements, and distributing maps and brochures. There are branches in train stations and airports as well. The phone number for tourist information in English is: 47208898. The office also has a fax number: 49525300.

The *Agence Nationale pour l'Information Touristique* will send you information by mail if you write to them at 8 Avenue de l'Opéra (75001). Of course, you can also contact the French Government Tourist Office in your own country.

EMBASSIES

Australia
4 Rue Jean-Rey (75015)
Metro: Bir Hakeim
Tel: 40593300
9am–5.30pm Monday to Friday

Canada
(Embassy and Consulate)
35 Ave Montaigne (75008)
Metro: Franklin Roosevelt or
Alma Marceau
Tel: 47230101
9am–4.30pm Monday to Friday

Denmark
77 Ave Marceau (75016)
Tel: 47203266

Ireland
4 Rue Rude (75016)
Tel: 45002087

Israel
3 Rue Rabelais (75008)
Tel: 42564747

Malaysia
32 Rue Spontini (75016)
Tel: 45531185

Netherlands
7 Rue Eblé (75007)
Tel: 43066188

New Zealand
(Embassy and Consulate)
7 Rue Léonard-de-Vinci (75016)

Metro: Victor Hugo
Tel: 45002411
Singapore
12 Ave Foch (75016)
Tel: 45003361

Sweden
17 Rue Barbet de Jouy (75007)
Tel: 45559215

United Kingdom
(Embassy) 35 Rue Fbg St Honoré
(75008)
(Consulate) 2 Rue d'Anjou (75008)
Metro: Concorde or Madeleine
Tel: 42669142
9am–5.30pm Monday to Friday

United States
(Embassy) 2 Avenue Gabriel (75008)
(Consulate) 2 Rue St Florentin
(75001)
Tel: 42961202 Metro: Concorde
9am–6pm Monday to Friday

Russia
79 Rue de Grenelle (75007)
Tel: 45489928

de Gaulle, Charles 17, 19
Debussy, Claude 16
Delacroix, Eugène 26, 72, 99
discos 65
Dubuffet, Jean 34
duty free regulations 80–1

Acknowledgments

Photography by

6/7, 10/11 Ping Amranand

17T & B Archiv Für Kunst und geschichte, Berlin

16, 20, 23T & B, 25, 26T, 30, 31B, 32T, 33, 35, 36, 38T & B, 40T & B, 41, 42, 46T & B, 48T, 50, 53B, 54, 55, 56T, 58T, 59, 61, 63T & B, 64, 65T & B, 66, 67T, 69T, 71, 72, 74, 75T & B, 76, 77T & B, 78, 79, 81, 83, 92, 95, 100T Guy Bourdíer

13, 18, 22, 29, 34, 39, 47, 48B, 51, 52, 53T, 56B, 60, 68, 69B, 70, 80, 82, 84, 85T & B, 86, 87, 88, 89T & B, 91, 93T & B, 94T & B, 96, 97T & B, 98, 99, 100B, 101 Annabel Elston

12, 15T Musées de la Ville de Paris

5, 21, 24T & B, 26B, 27, 28, 31T, 32B, 35T, 37, 43T & B, 49, 58B, 67B, 73, 90 Bill Wassman

Handwriting V Barl
Cover Design Klaus Geisler
Cartography Berndtson & Berndtson

INSIGHT GUIDES

COLORSET NUMBERS

You'll find the colorset number on the spine of each Insight Guide.

INSIGHT *pocket* GUIDES

United States: Houghton Mifflin Company, Boston MA 02108
Tel: (800) 2253362 Fax: (800) 4589501

Canada: Thomas Allen & Son, 390 Steelcase Road East
Markham, Ontario L3R 1G2
Tel: (416) 4759126 Fax: (416) 4756747

Great Britain: GeoCenter UK, Hampshire RG22 4BJ
Tel: (256) 817987 Fax: (256) 817988

Worldwide: Höfer Communications Singapore 2262
Tel: (65) 8612755 Fax: (65) 8616438

" I was first drawn to the Insight Guides by the excellent "Nepal" volume. I can think of no book which so effectively captures the essence of a country. Out of these pages leaped the Nepal I know – the captivating charm of a people and their culture. I've since discovered and enjoyed the entire Insight Guide Series. Each volume deals with a country or city in the same sensitive depth, which is nowhere more evident than in the superb photography. "

Sir Edmund Hillary

NOTES